# Toward a Sincere Prayer



Shaykh Ḥabīb al-Kāẓimī

al-Burāq

# Copyright



ISBN: 978-1-956276-73-2
Printed and published by al-Burāq Publications.
Translated and annotated by al-Burāq Publications. Where needed, context and transliterations were added. Some minor edits were made to the translated Arabic text.



al-Buraq.org
info@al-Buraq.org

First Edition | December 2025

# Dedication

The publication of this book was made possible through the generous support of our donors.

Please recite *Sūrat al-Fātihah* and ask God for the Divine reward (*thawāb*) to be conferred upon the donors and also the souls of all the deceased in whose memory their loved ones have contributed graciously towards the publication of *Toward a Sincere Prayer.*

We begin by giving all praise and thanks to God ﷻ for giving us the *tawfiq* to translate this book. He has guided us and without Him, we would not have been guided to the straight path embodied by the Prophet Muḥammad ﷺ and the Ahl al-Bayt عليهم السلام.

This book is dedicated to all the scholars, martyrs and believers who worked tirelessly to promote the pure Muḥammadan path.

We want to also give our thanks and appreciation to all believers from around the world and acknowledge the team which helped al-Burāq Publications complete this work, spending countless hours to make its publication possible. Please recite Sūrat al-Fātiḥah on behalf of them, their families, and their marḥūmīn.

# Duʿāʾ al-Ḥujjah

اللهم كن لوليك الحجة بن الحسن صلواتك
عليه وعلى آبائه في هذه الساعة وفي كل
ساعة وليا وحافظا وقائدا وناصرا ودليلا
وعينا حتى تسكنه أرضك طوعا وتمتعه فيها طويلا

O God, be, for Your representative, the Ḥujjat (proof), son of al-Ḥasan, Your blessings be upon him and his forefathers, in this hour and in every hour: a guardian, a protector, a leader, a helper, a proof, and an eye—until You make him live on the Earth, in obedience (to You), and cause him to live in it for a long time.

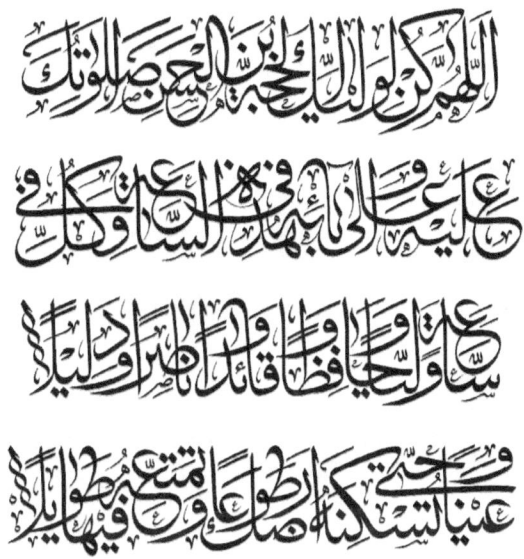

# Terms of Respect

The following Arabic phrases have been used throughout this book in their respective places to show the reverence which the noble personalities deserve.

عزّ وجلّ

Used for God, meaning:
*Exalted and Sublime (Perfect) is He*

صلى الله عليه وآله

Used for Prophet Muḥammad, meaning:
*Blessings from God be upon him and his family*

عليه السلام

Used for a man (singular) of a high status, meaning:
*Peace be upon him*

عليها السلام

Used for a woman (singular) of a high status, meaning:
*Peace be upon her*

عليهما السلام

Used for men/women (dual) of a high status, meaning:
*Peace be upon them both*

عليهم السلام

Used for men and/or women (plural) of a high status, meaning:
*Peace be upon them all*

عجّل الله تعالى فرجه الشريف

Used for Imām Muḥammad al-Mahdī, meaning:
*May God hasten his return*

قدّس سرّه

Used for a deceased scholar, meaning:
*May his resting [burial] place remain pure*

# Transliteration Table

The method of transliteration of Islāmic terminology from the Arabic language has been carried out according to the standard transliteration table below.

| | | | | | |
|---|---|---|---|---|---|
| ء | ʾ | ر | r | ف | f |
| ا | a | ز | z | ق | q |
| ب | b | س | s | ك | k |
| ت | t | ش | sh | ل | l |
| ث | th | ص | ṣ | م | m |
| ج | j | ض | ḍ | ن | n |
| ح | ḥ | ط | ṭ | و | w |
| خ | kh | ظ | ẓ | ه | h |
| د | d | ع | ʿ | ي | y |
| ذ | dh | غ | gh | | |
| **Long Vowels** | | | | | |
| ا | ā | و | ū | ي | ī |
| **Short Vowels** | | | | | |
| ـَ | a | ـُ | u | ـِ | i |

# Table of Contents

# Publisher's Introduction

بسم الله الرحمن الرحيم

*In the Name of God, the Beneficent, the Merciful*

Amid technological advancements and a multitude of social media platforms, the reader has become in desperate need of reliable sources from which they can obtain intellectual enrichment represented by written publications, which continue to hold the lead position for the educated person. The task of providing these reliable foundations and academic sources is a responsibility that must be tackled with care to preserve the intellectual heritage, advance the educational presentation, and present it in its simplest and grandest forms to the dear reader.

And so, Nūr al-Maʿārif Institute has taken up this responsibility by undertaking the publication of the ethical and religious books needed by the dear reader, especially in this time, in which book compositions have increased and publication sources have multiplied, leaving the reader lost in front of thousands of printed titles, without a dependable academic supervisor that carries the moral obligation of providing an academic basis for the dear readers.

Nūr al-Maʿārif Institute's method of connecting with the dear reader is illustrated by its integrity, as it presents reliable books and academic endowments rooted in the doctrine of Ahl al-Bayt عليهم السلام, under diligent supervision and review of everything the published book contains. This season, we provide the dear reader with a bouquet of new titles, presented with an articulate presentation that the reader will enjoy and draw from its treasures to his capacity.

Between the reader's hands lies this collection of works by the virtuous educator, Shaykh Ḥabīb al-Kāẓimī, with the following titles: *Mahdawī Inspirations*; *Toward a Happy Family*; *The Daily Program for the Pure Believers*; *Toward the Love of Imām al-Ḥusayn* عليه السلام; and *Toward a Sincere Prayer*. We also promise the dear reader that we will provide more ethical and academic publications from Nūr al-Maʿārif Institute. We ask the Lord to make us among those who carry the torch of the ideology of Prophet Muḥammad ﷺ to its seekers, and hope to live up to the expectations of the dear reader.

Nūr al-Maʿārif Publications

# Author's Introduction

بسم الله الرحمن الرحيم

*In the Name of God, the Beneficent, the Merciful*

There are many books written about the manners of a meaningful prayer and the narrations concerning it. In this book, however, we wish to summarise what we mentioned in our book *The Secrets of Prayer*, so that it can be a companion to the believer on this Divine journey and a part of his prayer mat, at his reach whenever the chance arises. Practical observance of the contents of an ascensive prayer is the first step to applying them, since the motivational narrations primarily, and the quotes of the scholars secondarily, really spark the eagerness to perform this ritual in the best form possible. This booklet's chapters have the same titles as the original book. However, some paragraphs have been shortened and summarised to be easily conveyed to lovers of reverent prayer.

I ask the God ﷻ to aid us in upholding what was made the pole of religion, to make it a worthy meeting, and a realistic ascension to Him.

Shaykh Ḥabīb al-Kāẓimī

Najaf, The Day of Ghadīr, 1440 AH

# The Etiquette of Preparing for Prayer

Worship has a majesty and an interior, and as Ḥajj is not simply visible actions performed by the pilgrims, nor is the core of prayer merely bodily actions. The narrations of the Prophet and his Household عليهم السلام indicate from afar—or rather, from up close—to this truth. And perhaps this thought-provoking narration highlights this very truth, where it is narrated that Amīr al-Mu'minīn, Imām 'Alī عليه السلام said:

> If the one who prays only knew how God's glory surrounds him during prayer, he would never raise his head after prostrating in worship.[1]

He who wants a sincere prayer must live in a state of yearning for entering the sea of prayer. And, one who wants to reach the majesty of prayer should certainly feel this sensation before the time of prayer, looking forward to it eagerly. The devout and pious prepare themselves to meet the Lord an hour or so beforehand, whereas the common people are surprised by the entry of prayer time. Perhaps some of them even wish, deep down inside, that the prayer time would not transpire, for it would ruin their entertainment, or whatever they are busy with in this world!

The major matters in life and their important meanings begin with indoctrination and become second nature

---

[1] Ṣadūq, Shaykh Muḥammad b. 'Alī, *al-Khiṣāl*, Vol. 2, Page 610.

through persistent practice. One should not tire of this continuous indoctrination, as the path to God ﷻ is an action contrary to human nature, which inclines him towards worldly cravings, sluggishness, prioritising soon over later, preferring pleasure over struggle, and ranking present benefits over future benefits. To summarise with an example, we say: one who wishes to swim against the current must initially struggle, suffer, and strain, until he becomes accustomed to riding the waves and overcoming obstacles.

Entering the sea of prayer requires prior self-preparation, meaning one should create a margin between oneself and prayer, like an isthmus between two worlds, because it is clear that one cannot usually leave the atmosphere in which they were living in a single moment. For example, if a man were quarrelling with his wife, then, if he entered into prayer, he would naturally remain in a quarrel with her. Therefore, a worshipper must constantly praise God ﷻ before sunset and before sunrise, in a place in which he can prepare himself to stand before God ﷻ, and gradually depart the environment of interacting with the elements of this world.

One of the requirements for success and preparation for a submissive prayer is to watch one's actions between prayers. There is a beautiful expression in the books of ethics that states: he who covers himself with honey, then approaches the house of wasps, it is natural for the wasps to attack him and sting him in every part of his body, because the honey that he coated himself with attracts such wasps. By analogy with this example, the devils are attracted to such a disobedient person, preoccupied with his own pleasures and faults, and oblivious to it.

He who does not have a companion in life, nor a comforter, may live in a state of repression, distress, then eruption, followed by complete collapse. It has been observed in the narrations of Ahl al-Bayt ﷺ that they would retreat to prayer whenever they find themselves concerned by a certain matter or struck by a problem. And the believer must be like this, seeking refuge in prayer at all times and circumstances, whether it be in the middle of the night or the bright of day, at the market or in the home. Whenever he is at the height of anger and despair and gloom towards life, he finds himself in a corner in his house to speak with the Lord of the Worlds through the supplication of a desperate seeker.

If we were to exemplify the essence of prayer in a single verse, it would be the Almighty's words:

﴿إِنَّ ٱلصَّلَوٰةَ تَنۡهَىٰ عَنِ ٱلۡفَحۡشَآءِ وَٱلۡمُنكَرِ﴾

*﴿inna ṣ-ṣalāta tanhā ʿani l-faḥshāʾi wa-l-munkari﴾*

*﴿Indeed the prayer restrains from indecent and wrongful conduct﴾*[2]

---

[2] Sūrat al-ʿAnkabūt, Verse 45.

and so if the prayer does not prevent indecency and evil, it is not a prayer, or it is an incomplete prayer missing its properties and effects, and things are pursued specifically for their properties, just like effective medicines. Therefore, if one wants to know of his prayers' acceptance by his Lord, he must view the effect of his prayer on his daily life, especially at the moment of the desire to sin. Should his prayer prevent him from sinning, he would be an upholder of the truth of prayer and a fulfiller of it in the progression of his life.

One of the things that truly points out to us the greatness of prayer is the Almighty's phrase:

﴿وَٱسْتَعِينُوا۟ بِٱلصَّبْرِ وَٱلصَّلَوٰةِ ۚ وَإِنَّهَا لَكَبِيرَةٌ إِلَّا عَلَى ٱلْخَـٰشِعِينَ﴾

﴿*wa-sta'īnū bi-ṣ-ṣabri wa-ṣ-ṣalāti wa-'innahā la-kabīratun illā 'alā l-khāshi'īna*﴾

﴿*And take recourse in patience and prayer, and it is indeed hard except for the humble*﴾[3]

The verse's implication is clear, but there are a few points to contemplate. Here are some of them:

What made the prayer so close to the soul and easy on it is none other than the state of reverence and acceptance.

[3] Sūrat al-Baqarah, Verse 45.

A reverent person is the one who lives with this attribute in a permanent state, so that reverence becomes his nature. Otherwise, veneration in a passing moment and a temporary context, such as being at a holy site, is not a noteworthy achievement.

One of the verses that indicates the outcome of the prayer is His phrase:

﴿وَأَقِمِ ٱلصَّلَوٰةَ لِذِكۡرِيٓ﴾

﴿*wa-'aqimi ṣ-ṣalāta li-dhikrī*﴾

﴿*and maintain the prayer for My remembrance*﴾[4]

for it designated remembrance as the purpose of prayer, and in this respect, the solely physical prayer that lacks remembrance—and is a state of the body and limbs—lacks the purpose of its legislation. An example of this in the visible world is the doctor. When the doctor tells his patient to buy medicine in the hope of a cure, his purpose is not simply the purchase of the medicine, but the cure that follows. Otherwise, if he knows the medicine has no effect, he would not intend for the purchase to happen at all.

Success in all daily activities in all their dimensions relies on a sincere prayer, just like the words of Imām ʿAlī ﵇:

---

[4] Sūrat Ṭā Hā, Verse 14.

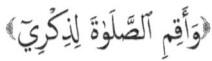

> And know that all of your deeds follow your prayer. So, whoever is negligent of his prayer will be more negligent in other acts.[5]

Therefore, whoever connects his own existence to the higher level of existence in every aspect would naturally be acknowledged by his Lord with all the varieties of blessings. An example of this is Tawbah, as mentioned in the holy verse:

﴿ثُمَّ تَابَ عَلَيۡهِمۡ لِيَتُوبُوٓاْ﴾

﴾*thumma tāba ʿalayhim li-yatūbū*﴿

﴾*then He turned clemently toward them so that they might be penitent*﴿[6]

So just as the servant's repentance lies between two penitences, the servant's piety is between two devotions; the Lord accepts the servant generally, and by the blessings of this attention, the servant accepts his Lord, in return for which the abundant acceptance of the Lord is achieved.

He who loves conversation with a beloved who does not know his language will certainly strive vigorously to solve the ambiguity in the language of communication to attain the pleasure of talking to his beloved. And here we must

---

[5] Mufīd, Shaykh Muḥammad, *al-Amālī*, p. 260.

[6] Sūrat at-Tawbah, Verse 118.

say that, whoever wants this delightful exchange with his Lord must learn the manner of dialogue and its vocabulary, which is something attainable only through a sincere prayer, which is the ascending Qur'ān, just as the sociable conversation of the Lord with His servant is expressed in the descending Qur'ān.

There is a torment that everybody will go through, throughout the Barzakh and Baʿth, in addition to the stages of the Day of Judgement—everyone except the Prophets and Infallibles, of course—which is the torment that follows the person from the night of his burial until the moment he enters Heaven. This is the destructive desperation that, should it remain within the servant, nobody would feel the pleasure of entering Heaven. And one of the greatest examples of this desperation is the despair that results from not perfecting the prayers that occupy the days of this worldly life and not improving their performance, despite progress in many other aspects of his life, such as money, family, and so forth.

Doubts during the prayer have clear jurisprudential solutions, such as adding an extra rakʿah as a precaution after the prayer. However, it is unacceptable for the believer who is attentive to his prayer to be caught in a state of doubt and uncertainty, because of the different emotional colours in each of the rakʿahs of prayer:

In the first rakʿah, the yearning is one's conversation with the Lord of the Worlds in the first moments of the interaction.

In the second rakʿah: A station of supplication with God ﷻ.

In the third rakʿah: Remembrance of the feeling of sincerity during qunūt, along with a tear that has not yet dried.

In the fourth rakʿah: The scent of farewell, accompanied by the sadness and gloom it creates.

God ﷻ says in His Holy Book:

﴿فَوَيْلٌ لِّلْمُصَلِّينَ﴾

﴿*fa-waylun li-l-muṣallīn*[a]﴾

﴿ٱلَّذِينَ هُمْ عَن صَلَاتِهِمْ سَاهُونَ﴾

﴿[a]*lladhīna hum ʿan ṣalātihim sāhūn*[a]﴾

﴿*Woe to those who pray but are heedless of their prayers*﴾[7]

These are truly frightening verses to those who understand and comprehend; He made the subject of the threat the one who prays, so what is meant by a heedless person? There are a few possible meanings:

---

[7] Sūrat al-Māʿūn, Verses 4–5.

The person who is distracted during his prayer, as happens to many worshippers, and the woe meant here would imply exclusion and loss.

The person who is intermittent in his prayers; he prays one day and neglects the other, as highlighted by the woe in its literal sense that promises a dreadful punishment that suits the negligence of prayer, even if only sometimes.

The person who abandons prayer completely at all times, and this person is the ultimate example of the word "heedless".

One of the reasons for sincerity whilst in front of God ﷻ is the comprehension of the eminence of the One before Whom we stand. It is narrated, according to some of the wives of the Prophet ﷺ:

> The Prophet ﷺ would discuss with us, and we would discuss with him, but whenever prayer presented, it is as if he did not even know us, and we did not know him.[8]

So the Prophet ﷺ, despite his sympathy towards all of creation and his utmost care for his family, whenever the time for meeting his Lord would arrive, he would divert his entire being away from creation towards the One whom he

[8] Majlisī, 'Allāmah Muḥammad Bāqir, *Biḥār al-Anwār*, Vol. 67, p. 400.

would look forward to all day to meet. Hence, prayer to him was like a station for meeting his beloved.

When some people in this world prepare to meet a worldly sovereign, they are so taken aback by humility that they cannot speak properly, but when it comes to standing before the Supreme Lord, we do not feel this humility. This is caused by the veil of obscurity enshrouding all of us. However, it is known that if this veil were lifted from our hearts, we would witness from His majesty that which would achieve this humility, suiting that majesty which no majesty surpasses. As a witness to this principle, it is narrated that Imām Zayn al-ʿĀbidīn ﷺ said:

> And should I turn my face from Him, He would turn His face from me, so who would be seen as merciful after Him?[9]

The famous phrase describing prayer as "the believer's ascension" clearly indicates that prayer involves a process of flying and soaring to the higher skies in the World of Meaning. Otherwise, pretending to be like the soarers does not achieve any degree of transcendence at all. It is comparable to a person who goes to the airport, boards the plane, and sits in it without it flying, gets off the plane, and heads back home. Can he say he travelled to the destination he left for?! Similarly, the mosques are like airports, and our prayers are like aeroplanes. If we do not achieve a spiritual

[9] Ibid., Vol. 81, p. 245.

voyage within them, there is no voyage, nor airport, nor aeroplane!

He who intends to travel to God ﷻ must have a travel plan; otherwise, the more he travels, the farther away he becomes. And undoubtedly, one of the most important requirements in this plan is establishing the prayer, not merely performing it deprived of the meanings that achieve its actual establishment. Establishing the prayer differs from simply performing it, like the difference between an erected tent and one crumpled on the ground. Thus, the prayer is the pole for the tent of faith, for it is obvious that a crumpled tent on the ground neither protects its occupier from cold nor heat, unless erected upon its poles.

A sincere prayer is of the greatest projects in the world of creation, for it is a building above all buildings; rather, it is like building one of the highest and most expensive towers on the face of the Earth. And it should be known that these multiple rakʿahs require a plan and programme, as do the towers in this finite world. Just as the person who succeeds in building one floor is then able to make the rest of the floors similar to it, so he who masters one rakʿah can master all of his prayers with all of their perfected rakʿahs.

Some of us traverse the route towards God ﷻ based upon tastes, upon likes and dislikes, so they pray Ṣalāt al-Layl for a while, then abandon it, and recite the Qurʾān for some time, then leave it. Thus, a person will never reach a safe zone. Rather, he should take a moment and say to himself:

> We have not enjoyed the indulgences of the people of this world, not even the permissible ones, after we experienced something of the pleasures of the afterlife, which amaze us more than any other pleasures. And on the other hand, we have not reached anything noteworthy from the pleasures of the World of Meaning.

Hence, prayer can be taken as a focal point to establish the centre of that Lordly light initially, then gradually expand it to include the interval between two prayers.

One of the main purposes of the mustaḥabb parts of prayer and other worship is to connect the worshipper to what gives him a special proximity to the Lord of Reverence and Majesty, in addition to the general proximity he gains from the actual prayer.

Hence, he who maintains these mustaḥabb parts—which involve most of the parts of prayer—places his prayer in the distinguished circle of acceptance. It is as if God ﷻ created an additional way for His special devotees to approach Him, so that when they perform the mustaḥabb, it is accompanied by eagerness and yearning to attain that special proximity to God, not simply to complete their assignment and earn some privileges.

Shayṭān distracts some by saying:

> Since you are overwhelmed by sins and wrongdoings anyway, what is the point of performing a prayer that does not prevent indecencies and wrongs?!

The answer to this Shayṭānic goading is that: The bodily presentation of prayer can be a step towards the true representation of prayer, just like a person hanging by a thin thread inside of a well does not cut that thread, claiming that it is useless! And the witness to this is what was narrated, that a young man from the Anṣār would pray with the Prophet ﷺ and still commit indecencies. When this was described to the Prophet ﷺ, he said:

> His prayer will prevent him one day.[10]

And he soon repented.

If a servant is brought on the Day of Judgement, and his deeds are shown to him, and he sees nothing in his list of deeds. Still, two sincere accepted rakʿahs—when his virtuous deeds and bad deeds are equal to each other—this prayer would be sufficient to enter him into Heaven forever. How great the sincere prayer must be to have the power to provide eternal joy for the servant! And this is understood from the narration of Prophet ﷺ:

> When you stand for prayer, face [the qiblah], recite the Mother of the Book (meaning Sūrat al-Fātiḥah) and

[10] Ibid., Vol. 79, p. 198.

> what is easy for you from the chapters, bow and perfect your bowing and prostrating, testify, and recite the taslīm, then every sin you have committed between each prayer will be forgiven.[11]

He who wishes to achieve a reverent prayer must begin by deepening the element of knowledge within his existence. The more he knows about the degrees of lordship, the closer he becomes to the circle of attraction towards God. He, therefore, is showered with the lights of His love and affection to the extent that the lover does not bear being late to prayer due to the excitement towards the joy and delight that the meeting holds. And this is what we understand from one Infallible's description of another, as narrated that Imām Ja'far aṣ-Ṣādiq ﷺ said:

> By God, 'Alī b. al-Ḥusayn used to recognise the One before Whom he was standing.[12]

A person experiences states of laziness, sluggishness, and deterrence, and it is known that the rhythm of the prayer during these times is one of the reasons for not performing a sincere prayer. And so, the servant must choose a time in which he clears himself of all the factors of deterrence from worship, and this is the advice of Amīr al-Mu'minīn ﷺ when he said:

---

[11] Ṣadūq, Shaykh Muḥammad b. 'Alī, *al-Amālī*, p. 549.

[12] al-Ḥurr al-'Āmilī, Shaykh Muḥammad, *Wasā'il al-Shī'ah*, Vol. 5, p. 474.

> You should not do your prayers lazily or sleepily, nor think about yourself, for you are between the hands of your Honourable, Exalted Lord. And as for one's prayer, whatever He accepts from him is what was from the heart.[13]

Regardless of how much effort a servant puts into perfecting his deeds, he will find himself on the Day of Judgement with many errors that cause his good deeds to be rejected, in addition to which the major inexcusable flaw in the vast majority of his work will be exposed. Hence, he must find a way to achieve God's mercy through His means, one of which is the intercession of His servants during the events of the Day of Judgement. However, it should be known that this intercession is only attained by those outside the circle of slackness towards the prayer. And what is interesting is that this warning was the final narration from Imām Ja'far aṣ-Ṣādiq ﷺ, as Imām Mūsā al-Kāẓim ﷺ narrates:

> When my father was approaching death, he said to me,
>
> > O my son, our intercession will not apply to those who take their prayer lightly.[14]

One of the many blessings of a sincere prayer is the envelopment of the worshipper in a cloak of glory and

---

[13] Ibid., p. 477.

[14] Kulaynī, Shaykh Muḥammad b. Ya'qūb, *al-Kāfī*, Vol. 3, p. 270.

splendour, making the devils afraid to approach him. God would then watch over the servant, and Shayṭān would not dare approach somebody whom God ﷻ has guaranteed to protect, just as He confirmed when He said:

﴿إِنَّ ٱللَّهَ يُدَٰفِعُ عَنِ ٱلَّذِينَ ءَامَنُوٓا۟﴾

﴾*inna llāha yudāfiʿu ʿani lladhīna āmanū*﴿

﴾*God will indeed defend those who have faith*﴿[15]

And the opposite is also true. He who neglects his prayers is targeted by Shayṭān when the protection is lifted from him. And this is what the Prophet ﷺ explained by saying:

> Shayṭān continues to be afraid of a believing person as long as he protects his five daily prayers, but when he loses them, Shayṭān becomes daring, then he takes him into great sins.[16]

Some people wish to know their position with the Almighty Lord, and whether He is pleased with them or disappointed with them?! Here is the role of prayer in revealing a person's reality and how close he is to his Lord, as it is a meeting with God ﷻ. So if the meeting was marked by eagerness and affection, the close relationship of those involved becomes apparent. Imām Jaʿfar aṣ-Ṣādiq ؑ made a

---

[15] Sūrat al-Ḥajj, Verse 38.

[16] Kulaynī, Shaykh Muḥammad b. Yaʿqūb, *al-Kāfī*, Vol. 3, Page 269.

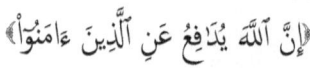

person's performance of prayer as the basis of praise and flattery, where the narrator says:

> Once, I spoke before Abū ʿAbd Allāh (Imām Jaʿfar aṣ-Ṣādiq ﷺ) about a man of our people, and I praised him well. The Imām asked,
>
> > How is his prayer?[17]

He who wants a sincere prayer through perfume, clean clothes, and even attending jamāʿah in the mosque, in addition to other supplements to prayer, must know that the aforementioned actions do not necessarily entail performance of a sincere prayer; for there is a need for hard work on purifying the heart that is in the reach of the Devil that is floating around it. And this purification is not accomplished except through constant vigilance to achieve the presence of God ﷻ on the one hand, and to control what is ensuing within the spirit on the other hand.

Prayer is an integral combination, in the sense that it includes several essential ingredients to nourish the human spirit, for it contains:

Glorification of God ﷻ, by remembering His majesty and splendour that minds cannot comprehend, through the adhān and iqāmah.

---

[17] Ibid., p. 487.

Recitation of the Book of God ﷻ, where there is an obligatory chapter, which is Sūrat al-Fātiḥah, and an optional chapter.

The station of duʿāʾ, which is qunūt, where the worshipper can supplicate for whatever he wishes.

The request for blessings upon the Prophet ﷺ, and this is through the recurring intonation during adhān, iqāmah, rukūʿ, sujūd, tashahhud, and taslīm.

The legislation of prayer is an ancient law that spans the history of the Prophets ﷺ. Witness to this is that when God ﷻ ordered Prophet Mūsā ﷺ to communicate religion to his people, He said to him:

﴿وَأَقِمِ ٱلصَّلَوٰةَ لِذِكْرِيٓ﴾

﴾*wa-ʾaqimi ṣ-ṣalāta li-dhikrī*﴿

﴾*and maintain the prayer for My remembrance*﴿[18]

He made prayer the basis of God's remembrance. Likewise, the narration of Prophet Ibrāhīm ﷺ is testimony to this, as he said:

﴿رَبِّ ٱجْعَلْنِي مُقِيمَ ٱلصَّلَوٰةِ﴾

---

[18] Sūrat Ṭā Hā, Verse 14.

﴾*rabbi jʿalnī muqīma ṣ-ṣalāti*﴿

﴾*My Lord! Make me a maintainer of prayer*﴿[19]

and also what was said about Prophet Ismāʿīl ﵇:

﴿وَكَانَ يَأۡمُرُ أَهۡلَهُۥ بِٱلصَّلَوٰةِ﴾

﴾*wa-kāna yaʾmuru ahlahū bi-ṣ-ṣalāti*﴿

﴾*He used to bid his family to [maintain] the prayer*﴿[20]

and what Prophet ʿĪsā ﵇ said:

﴿وَأَوۡصَٰنِي بِٱلصَّلَوٰةِ﴾

﴾*wa-ʾawṣānī bi-ṣ-ṣalāti*﴿

﴾*and He has enjoined me to [maintain] the prayer*﴿[21]

and too is the universal instruction to Isrāʾīl's (meaning Prophet Yaʿqūb ﵇) progeny:

﴿وَأَقِيمُواْ ٱلصَّلَوٰةَ وَءَاتُواْ ٱلزَّكَوٰةَ﴾

---

[19] Sūrat Ibrāhīm, Verse 40.

[20] Sūrat Maryam, Verse 55.

[21] Sūrat Maryam, Verse 31.

﴾*wa-'aqīmū ṣ-ṣalāta wa-'ātū z-zakāta*﴿

﴾*And maintain the prayer, and give the zakat*﴿[22]

Prayer is the embodiment of the humility of servitude on the servant's side, and a manifestation of the glory of Lordship on the side of the Master. For through prayer, servitude is achieved on the one side, and Lordship is demonstrated on the other, just as Imām 'Alī ﷺ said:

> O my God! It is enough of an honor for me to be your slave. And it is enough of a source of pride for me that You are my Lord.[23]

Thus, if the worshipper observes himself, he feels the atmosphere of servitude to God ﷻ, and if he observes his Creator, he feels the magnificence of Lordship. Hence, the reverent worshipper fluctuates between these two colours throughout his prayer, and what a feeling it is!

When a feeling of distress and anguish strikes the people of this world, they seek refuge in what relieves them. It is known that the inside of a person is never eased by what is outside, because the lover of outer pleasures is only satisfied as long as he is distracted by those pleasures, in addition to the fact that worldly pleasures require factors that not

---

22 Sūrat al-Baqarah, Verse 83.

23 Majlisī, 'Allāmah Muḥammad Bāqir, *Biḥār al-Anwār*, Vol. 74, p. 400.

everyone can achieve. Meanwhile, the believer who has reached the stage of proximity to the truth sees all the pleasure in communicating with his greatest Beloved. And the Prophet ﷺ was at the peak of those who lived this sensation, as narrated in his speech to Abū Dharr:

> Oh Abū Dharr! God, glorious is His praise, has made the prayer the apple of my eye, and made it beloved to me, like food is made lovable to the hungry and water to the thirsty. And surely the hungry one, when he eats, he is satiated, and the thirsty one, when he drinks, he is quenched, but I am not satiated from prayer.[24]

Human nature leads a person to see his Lord as merely a means to satisfy his worldly needs. And there is no harm in the person employing this nature to connect himself to the unseen world, until he reaches the stage of being relieved of all mortal restrictions. From this perspective, a person can motivate himself to focus during prayer by recalling his pressing needs. And what points to this truth is the narration from Imām Jaʿfar aṣ-Ṣādiq عليه السلام, who said:

> When a man stands up for prayer but considers it insignificant, God, the Most Holy, the Most High, says to his angels,
>
> > Look at this servant of Mine. It seems as if he thinks his needs are in someone else's hands. Does

[24] Ibid., p. 73.

> he not know that meeting his needs is in My hand?[25]

However much effort the servant puts into guiding the bird of imagination to where he wants during prayer, he will find that it is a harder task than he thought, because the mind is fleeting and unpredictable, so it is impossible to control it using only willpower. Therefore, special metaphysical reinforcement is needed to assist the servant in bringing all the dimensions of his existence into his hand and under his control, including the body, heart, and mind. But the following narration offers hope regarding this duty, in which the Prophet ﷺ is reported to have said:

> God ﷻ said,
>
> > When I look at the heart of a bondsman, I know if he has sincere love and obedience for My sake and seeks My pleasure in it. Then I take charge of him and draw him closer.[26]

Fighting the distracting interruptions in prayer, as thinking of matters other than God ﷻ:

---

[25] al-Ḥurr al-ʿĀmilī, Shaykh Muḥammad, *al-Jawāhir al-Saniyyah fī al-Aḥādīth al-Qudsīyyah*, p. 663.

[26] Majlisī, ʿAllāmah Muḥammad Bāqir, *Biḥār al-Anwār*, Vol. 82, p. 136.

It is sometimes through individually contesting every single thought that comes up, and the situation of this worshipper is like he who drives out the noisy birds from the tree he is lying under using a stick, only for them to come back so that he must drive them out with another stick!

And it is sometimes through cutting off the source of commotion from its roots, so he cuts down the tree, at which point there are no branches and no noisy birds. And this is the situation of the close servants who have reached the stage of absolute devotion to Him, just as Amīr al-Mu'minīn 卷 beseeched his Lord for.

The rank of the prayer with God 卷 rises through a factor that is sometimes:

Related to the prayer itself, such as the perfection of the preparation and segments of the prayer, and sincerity throughout them.

Related to the worshipper: two worshippers may perform a single prayer on the same level, but the degree of proximity of one of the prayers may be multiple times that of the other, depending on the worshipper's proximity.

And this meaning cannot be understood except through the quotes narrated from the Infallibles 卷, some of which indicate marriage as a means, as narrated from Imām Ja'far aṣ-Ṣādiq 卷:

> Two rakʿahs performed by a married person are better than seventy rakʿahs performed by a non-married person.[27]

And there are others which state knowledge as a means, as it is narrated from the Prophet ﷺ:

> O Ali! Two rakʿahs, which the scholar prays, are superior to seventy rakʿahs prayed by the worshipper.[28]

Obligatory and mustaḥabb prayers are like different types of gems in the vaults of the Almighty Lord. Just like gems differ in colour, size, and shine, so do prayers; some of which have two rakʿahs like Fajr, or three like Maghrib, or four like ʿIshāʾ, and some have five rukūʿs like Ṣalāt al-Āyāt, or five qunūts like ʿĪd Prayer. Some others involve repeating Sūrah, like Ṣalāt al-Waḥshah, and some don't even require wuḍūʾ, such as Ṣalāt al-Mayyit or the recitation of a Sūrah like in Ṣalāt al-Layl. Some prayers are related to one of the Imāms, like the Ḥujjah Prayer, and some don't relate to any of the Infallibles, like the prayer of Jaʿfar al-Ṭayyār.

The best phrase that summarizes for us the secret to sincerity in prayer is what Imām al-Ḥusayn ؑ announced on the night of ʿĀshūrāʾ, where he addressed the enemy and declared:

---

[27] Ṣadūq, Shaykh Muḥammad b. ʿAlī, *Man Lā Yaḥḍuruh al-Faqīh*, Vol. 3, p. 384.

[28] Majlisī, ʿAllāmah Muḥammad Bāqir, *Biḥār al-Anwār*, Vol. 2, p. 25.

> I love the prayer.[29]

Whoever reaches this level of love for this Lordly intermission will certainly have all internal obstacles removed naturally, to achieve harmony between the servant and his Lord through the exchange of affection between them. And it is obvious that, with this kind of holy bond, sincerity comes naturally with prayer.

One of the special features of prayer, which is unique to it, is that it is never to be dropped under any circumstances, as it should be performed in all settings, to the extent that there are special prayers such as:

Prayer of the Drowning: As Shaykh Ṭūsī mentions,

> And the person swimming in the water prays when drowning or required to swim, facing the qiblah should he know it, or in front of him if not, and his rukūʿ should be lower than his sujūd.[30]

Prayer of the Unclothed: The narration from Imām Jaʿfar aṣ-Ṣādiq ﷺ says:

> I (the narrator) asked him about a group that prayed jamāʿah while unclothed.

---

[29] Sayyid b. Ṭāwūs, *al-Luhūf ʿalā Qatlā al-Tufūf*, p. 85.

[30] Ṭūsī, Shaykh Muḥammad b. Ḥasan, *Tahdhīb al-Ahkām fī Sharḥ al-Muqniʿah*, Vol. 3, p. 174.

He said:

> The leader leads them on his knees, and prays with them being seated, and he is seated.[31]

Prayer of the March and Pursuit: It is narrated that Imām Muḥammad al-Bāqir ؑ said:

> Amīr al-Mu'minīn ؑ, performed prayer during the night of the battle of Ṣiffīn, which is called 'Laylat al-Ḥarīr'. Their prayer of Ẓuhr, 'Aṣr, Maghrib, and 'Ishā' were only takbīr ('God is great beyond description'), tahlīl ('no one deserves worship except God'), Taḥmīd ('all praise belongs to God'), and supplications. That was their prayer, and they were not ordered to repeat their prayers.[32]

Prayer of the Sick: Where the worshipper prays lying down or on his side, according to specifications outlined in Fiqh.

Prophet Nūḥ's Prayer, or the Prayer of the Ship: In which the worshipper faces the qiblah, and turns as the ship turns. Imām Ja'far aṣ-Ṣādiq ؑ commented on this prayer, saying:

---

[31] al-Ḥurr al-'Āmilī, Shaykh Muḥammad, *Wasā'il al-Shī'ah*, Vol. 4, p. 450.

[32] Majlisī, 'Allāmah Muḥammad Bāqir, *Biḥār al-Anwār*, Vol. 86, p. 115.

> That is the Prayer of Nūḥ ﷺ. Would you not like to pray the Prayer of Nūḥ ﷺ?[33]

Prayer of the Imprisoned: It is narrated from Sumāʿah:

> I asked him (the Imām) about a man who is a captive of the polytheists. It is time for prayer, but they do not allow him to perform it. He (the Imām) said,
>
> > He should make gestures.[34]

Among the matters that truly concern the pure worshipper, driving his ambition, is to have a progeny that establishes the prayer. This is what Prophet Ibrāhīm ﷺ asked for his offspring when he said:

﴿رَّبَّنَآ إِنِّيٓ أَسۡكَنتُ مِن ذُرِّيَّتِي بِوَادٍ غَيۡرِ ذِي زَرۡعٍ عِندَ بَيۡتِكَ ٱلۡمُحَرَّمِ رَبَّنَا لِيُقِيمُواْ ٱلصَّلَوٰةَ﴾

*﴿rabbanā innī askantu min dhurriyyatī bi-wādin ghayri dhī zarʿin ʿinda baytika l-muḥarrami rabbanā li-yuqīmū ṣ-ṣalāta﴾*

---

[33] al-Ḥurr al-ʿĀmilī, Shaykh Muḥammad, *Wasāʾil al-Shīʿah*, Vol. 5, p. 506.

[34] Kulaynī, Shaykh Muḥammad b. Yaʿqūb, *al-Kāfī*, Vol. 3, p. 457.

*{Our Lord! I have settled part of my descendants in a barren valley, by Your sacred House, our Lord, that they may maintain the prayer}*[35]

So settling them beside the Sacred House, in a barren valley, was for the fulfilment of this lofty objective, in addition to his request for the status of "Imām" for his offspring when God ﷻ made him an Imām for the people. And it is in this context that jurisprudence has encouraged training children to pray before puberty, so that it does not suddenly burden them. It is narrated that Amīr al-Mu'minīn ؏ said:

> Teach your children how to pray, and question them about it when they become eight years old.[36]

The nature of humankind drives them to seek refuge with all that can be grasped by sense, which is why it is said that a person drowning will grab on to every piece of hay. In contrast, in reality, should they contemplate accurately, they would realise that the One with control over the heavens and the Earth is none other than the Lord of Creation, and so seeking refuge should be with Him only. And thus the believer would never find a dead end in his lifespan as long as he holds this undoubted belief. And this

---

[35] Sūrat Ibrāhīm, Verse 37.

[36] Ṭabrisī, Mīrzā Ḥusayn Nūrī, *Mustadrak al-Wasāʾil wa-Mustanbaṭ al-Masāʾil*, Vol. 15, p. 169.

requires no more than what Imām Jaʿfar aṣ-Ṣādiq ﵇ mentioned when he said:

> What prevents one of you, when sorrow enters upon him from the sorrows of the world, that he performs wuḍūʾ, then enters his Masjid and performs rukūʿ of two cycles and supplicates to God ﷻ during these? Have you not heard God saying:
>
> ﴿وَٱسۡتَعِينُواْ بِٱلصَّبۡرِ وَٱلصَّلَوٰةِ﴾
>
> ﴿*wa-staʿīnū bi-ṣ-ṣabri wa-ṣ-ṣalāti*﴾
>
> ﴿*And take recourse in patience and prayer*﴾[37] [38]

Although prayer is considered one of many good deeds and virtues, God made it equal to all of them combined, where He said:

﴿وَأَوۡحَيۡنَآ إِلَيۡهِمۡ فِعۡلَ ٱلۡخَيۡرَٰتِ وَإِقَامَ ٱلصَّلَوٰةِ﴾

﴿*wa-ʾawḥaynā ilayhim fiʿla l-khayrāti wa-ʾiqāma ṣ-ṣalāti*﴾

﴿*and We revealed to them [concerning] the performance of good deeds, the maintenance of prayers*﴾[39]

---

[37] Sūrat al-Baqarah, Verse 45.

[38] al-ʿAyyāshī, Muḥammad b. Masʿūd, *Tafsīr al-ʿAyyāshī*, Vol. 1, p. 43.

[39] Sūrat al-Anbiyāʾ, Verse 73.

This signifies, firstly, that prayer was a constant commandment in the jurisdictions of the previous Prophets, and secondly, that it equates all the other good deeds combined. In fact, good deeds that are to be accepted by God ﷻ are only accomplishable by the worshipper when he prays.

Prayer is divided into several parts, each consisting of multiple actions: standing, bowing, sitting, and prostrating. And each of these actions has been assigned its own special dhikr, which is referred to in the Prophet ﷺ's quote:

> Gabriel ﷺ ordered me to recite Qur'ān while standing, and to thank Him [God ﷻ] while bowing, and to praise Him while prostrating, and to supplicate to Him while sitting.[40]

It is as if God ﷻ wants his servant to remember Him in all his motions, whether during prayer or outside of it, which is also understood from His verse:

﴿ٱلَّذِينَ يَذۡكُرُونَ ٱللَّهَ قِيَٰمٗا وَقُعُودٗا وَعَلَىٰ جُنُوبِهِمۡ﴾

*﴾alladhīna yadhkurūna llāha qiyāman wa-quʿūdan wa-ʿalā junūbihim﴿*

[40] Majlisī, ʿAllāmah Muḥammad Bāqir, *Biḥār al-Anwār*, Vol. 90, p. 313.

﴾*Those who remember God standing, sitting, and lying on their sides*﴿[41]

as all of the human’s movements in his daily life are narrowed down to those mentioned in this blessed verse.

At every moment, Shayṭān is hovering around a person's heart, searching for a way in, especially during prayer. This is understood from the use of the present tense in the verse:

﴾ٱلَّذِي يُوَسْوِسُ فِي صُدُورِ ٱلنَّاسِ﴿

﴾*ᵃlladhī yuwaswisu fī ṣudūri n-nāsⁱ*﴿

﴾*who puts temptations into the breasts of humans*﴿[42]

Repelling this is solely through dhikr. And the ‘dhikr’ that eliminates Shayṭān’s deceptions only comes from the ‘pious’, leading to ‘enlightenment’. And this is why some people see no impact of dhikr in our lives, despite its plentifulness, because they didn't work on the receiver (the soul) to make it receptive to the catalyst (dhikr), whether in prayer or elsewhere.

Progression towards perfection requires a movement opposite to human nature, for humans naturally cling to the Earth and seek the safe route. Thus, leaving matters as

---

[41] Sūrat Āl ʿImrān, Verse 191.

[42] Sūrat an-Nās, Verse 5.

they are does not result in salvation, however much the person should wish so. An illustration of this is visible in prayer. One who has not worked on perfecting their prayer internally and externally will remain in the same state they were in when it was first required of them, which is what Imām Ja'far aṣ-Ṣādiq ﷺ warned of, when speaking to Ḥammād b. 'Īsā, saying:

> It is a shame for a man of your people who at the age of sixty or seventy cannot even perform one prayer according to its complete rules and manners.[43]

A worshipper may be fortunate to perform a sincere prayer at some level, hence being safeguarded from the hypocrisy that could ruin his deeds. Still, he could later be subject to self-conceit, which is to the distinguished worshippers a deadly trap laid by Shayṭān—common people with their few and unperfected deeds may not find in themselves a reason for this condition to occur inside of them. The solution to this condition is to think about the following: firstly, where is the guarantee of acceptance, and secondly, where is the guarantee that the success will last, and thirdly, how will the previous shortcomings be compensated?!

---

[43] Kulaynī, Shaykh Muḥammad b. Ya'qūb, *al-Kāfī*, Vol. 3, p. 311.

# The Inner Etiquettes of Purification

Purification is the first step to entering the sanctuary of a sincere prayer. For if one of us has not perfected cleansing himself, he would be violating the entry condition of prayer according to Islāmic law, which is 'ṭahārah' (purity). It is the same when someone commits an error in bathing, for example, which would result in a violation of their Ghusl. A person who is constantly in a state of purity will immediately feel a sense of internal darkness when his purification is eradicated. All it takes is for him to sense that he is prohibited from praying, or putting his hand on the writing of the Noble Qur'ān, or touching the Holy Names of God, and that he is forbidden to enter mosques. It is as if the person who has purified himself has taken permission of entry from his Lord, and can pray in his presence whenever he wishes to.

Wuḍū' has two parts: physical wuḍū', which involves pouring water over the body, and consists of two washes and two wipes, and spiritual wuḍū', in which the worshipper cleanses his soul. A person who performs all the manners and rituals of wuḍū' could be said to have prayed before they'd prayed, as in their heart was in a state of yearning and closeness before even entering prayer. The recommended du'ā' of wuḍū' prepare the person to enter the sanctity of prayer, and if they are recited sincerely, the water of their wuḍū' may even be mixed with tears from their eyes.

If a person were to be stained with sins between the prayers, they should not lose hope in the mercy of God ﷻ. Just as one can purify the self physically through Ghusl and wuḍū', one can also purify the self internally through Tawbah to God ﷻ. This is why we see within the du'ā' of wuḍū' an invitation to internal cleansing. So the person who makes wuḍū' with this intention, and recites the du'ā' properly, will end up merging both wuḍū's: the wuḍū' of the body, and the wuḍū' of the spirit.

Interaction with God ﷻ during prayer has several stages, just as when meeting a king in this world, one must pass through several rooms and halls before reaching the meeting place. Otherwise, he who approaches his prayer mat in the worst state of mind and preparation will not set sail in the seas of a sincere prayer. We can see how the Prophet ﷺ and the Imāms ﵈ would be in a state of prayer from the time of their wuḍū', when their faces would even change colour, as is narrated.

wuḍū' is, in reality, a reminder of the need for internal cleansing. This is because the prayer is like Ḥajj; just as every step and ritual in Ḥajj symbolises a deeper meaning, so does wuḍū'. Doesn't the command to cleanse one's body, clothing, and surroundings also invite us to purify our hearts before meeting God ﷻ?

Some of the situations in which we are told to do Ghusl include: Making ziyārah to Imām al-Ḥusayn ؑ even if from afar, performing the Prayer of the Needy, performing

Istikhārah Prayer, complaining to God ﷻ about oppression and suffering, asking for the alleviation of a predicament, seeking enthusiasm for worship, and especially for performing Ṣalāt al-Layl, performing the Prayer of Gratitude, performing istighfār and asking for forgiveness, and, for women, when they have put on perfume for somebody other than their spouse. Indeed, entering the shower on any day other than Friday, or when the person is not in the state of Janabah, without any of the previously mentioned intentions, is truly a waste, especially when all it requires is a simple intent of the heart.

The time it takes a person to enter the shower and wash themselves is time that can be used more efficiently for worship. They can question themselves while washing about how they would look lying in the mortuary's cleaning room, as the two places share the same lack of clothing. They can question themselves about how they would be if they were sentenced to entering Hellfire, as the two places share similarity in the heat, even though the heat of the shower is incomparable to the heat of Hellfire.

The places where we are told not to relieve ourselves tell us much about the importance of upholding others' rights and avoiding actions that could harm others. We have been told to avoid water sources, open roads, residential areas, and even animal burrows. If servitude necessitates this amount of care in the simple act of relieving oneself, what about in the rest of life's serious undertakings?

It is important to be careful while making wuḍū' or Ghusl, so as not to exceed the required amount of care and fall into obsession, as the one who goes too far in cleansing himself is like one who invalidates it, according to what is narrated. Although this occurs in a state of obedience to God ﷻ, it is caused by none other than Shayṭān himself. Not only does obsessiveness lead to a waste of time and water, but it can also lead the servant to feel repulsion toward worship, which is the first step toward abandoning worship altogether, and may even lead the person to doubt their own faith. The cause of this illness is one. We are told not to put ourselves in such a vulnerable position.

# The Inner Etiquettes of Attire

The attire worn during prayer must be Mubāḥ, meaning not inappropriate. This means it should not be taken by force from another person by theft or such, nor should it have a legal payment due on it, such as Khums. The spiritual moral of this condition is that the Lord wants his servant to be exempt of all material liabilities between him and others, because any violation is an injustice committed by the person in his relationship with God or His servants, and how can one meet God ﷻ in a garment that is detested by Him, even if only on the account of a single strand of it?

A male servant should not wear gold or silk, as they are considered attire of luxury and softness, and are exclusively worn by women. The man, on the other hand, should show diligence and seriousness in life, and should therefore avoid wearing gold and silk both while praying and otherwise. The spiritual moral here is to get used to life's toughness and to avoid self-embellishment. It is narrated that Imām ʿAlī ؑ once said:

> Remember that the tree of the forest is the best timber, while green twigs have soft bark, and the wild bushes are very strong for burning, and slow in dying.[44]

Our Lord Almighty ordered His Prophet ﷺ to cleanse his clothing when He said:

﴿وَثِيَابَكَ فَطَهِّرْ﴾

---

[44] Sharīf Raḍī, Muḥammad b. al-Ḥusayn, *Nahj al-Balāghah*, p. 418.

﴾*wa-thiyābaka fa-ṭahhir*﴿

﴾*and purify your clothes*﴿[45]

If this command were metaphorical, it would mean that one must rectify his deeds, doing good to cleanse his spirit, for he is in relation to his spirit similar to what clothes are to the body. On the other hand, if it was meant literally, it means it is obligatory to be clean while praying, just as we are commanded to recite takbīr before prayer. So God ﷻ requests His servant not to approach Him with soiled clothes. And praying with even a patch of blood on one's clothes is inexcusable, let alone if his soul is filthy and covered in what is worse than visible grime. Thus, we can learn from the command to cleanse one's clothes that a person is required to purify his heart, and only then can he achieve the ascension he desires in prayer.

Another condition for the clothing worn during prayer is that it must cover the worshipper's private parts. The worshipper also has areas of shame inside his soul, which are the deficient spiritual states that the Compassionate Lord has covered with His kindness. But the human being, in his foolishness and unwise actions, reveals his inner privacies through the work of his body, and becomes just like a person with no clothing. These inner vulnerabilities can be erased, however, and this is where the high status lies, not in simply covering them up, so that if he were to

[45] Sūrat al-Muddaththir, Verse 4.

reveal his inner essence to others, it would be a beauty to look at. This exposure will occur on the Day of Judgment, whether the person likes it or not.

Within the narrations of the Prophet ﷺ Ahl al-Bayt عليهم السلام, we find a noteworthy emphasis on perfume, and a correlation may exist between perfume and the realm of the souls. We see that the person's soul is calmed when he applies perfume, and this may even extend to the angels around the worshipper. And what a victory it must be to multiply the reward for your prayer by seventy times, just by applying a small amount of perfume! This is what is narrated: Imām Jaʿfar aṣ-Ṣādiq عليه السلام said,

> Performing one prayer with perfume is better than seventy prayers without perfume.[46]

Islām has advocated for the use of Siwāk in numerous narrations, such as in the saying of the Prophet ﷺ:

> Were it not to cause hardship for my followers, I would have commanded them to brush their teeth for every prayer.[47]

Or his saying:

[46] Kulaynī, Shaykh Muḥammad b. Yaʿqūb, *al-Kāfī*, Vol. 6, p. 510.

[47] Ibid., Vol. 3, p. 22.

> Cleanse your mouths with Siwāk.[48]

We have been told to brush our teeth several times during the day and night, such as before going to sleep, after waking up, after every wuḍū', and after every prayer. And from all of this, not only do we understand how important it is not to approach the Lord with foul breath, but we also realise the importance of bodily health in general. It is medically proven that the mouth is the main access to the body, and that through the mouth, any filth can make its way into the body. Therefore, it is necessary to keep this area clean and sanitary, which is done through brushing the teeth.

---

[48] Pāyanda, Abū al-Qāsim, *Nahj al-Faṣāḥa*, p. 560.

# The Inner Mysteries of the Qiblah

It is only proper that the worshipper should search for the secrets of facing the qiblah, whether in general, such as when sleeping, or when sitting, or during the final throes of death, or in specific cases, such as the time of prayer. The qiblah has its secrets, just as the Kaʿbah has its rules, for God ﷻ gives special regard to the pilgrim walking around the Kaʿbah, and to those facing it during prayer. And even though it is known that

﴿فَأَيْنَمَا تُوَلُّوا۟ فَثَمَّ وَجْهُ ٱللَّهِ﴾

﴿*fa-'aynamā tuwallū fa-thamma wajhu llāhi*﴾

﴿*so whichever way you turn, there is the face of God*﴾[49]

The Almighty still orders us to look towards the Holy Mosque during our prayers.

When a worshipper prays to his Almighty Lord, he is effectively anchoring himself in a specific direction in this life. Just as he is physically directing himself to a particular location in this material realm, which is the "Ancient House" (the Kaʿbah), he must also direct his heart towards the owner of the House. But how should a person whose mind is scattered, such that he is engrossed in Dunyā one day and concerned with Ākhirah the next day, direct

---

[49] Sūrat al-Baqarah, Verse 115.

himself towards God ﷻ when his concern and thoughts are so dispersed? Therefore, the worshipper must establish within his heart a focal point to which he turns during the turbulences of life, as is narrated from Imām Jaʿfar aṣ-Ṣādiq ؑ:

> The heart is the sanctuary of God, so do not let settle in the sanctuary of God other than God.[50]

The eyes cannot observe God ﷻ. However, humans are drawn to material things because that is what they are made of. Therefore, God ﷻ gave the Kaʿbah to worshippers, a material symbol to which they can turn during their prayers. But the elite servants ascend beyond the material Kaʿbah and experience the beauty of proximity to the One whom the senses cannot reach.

When the worshipper stands up to pray, he says what he is taught by the Noble Qur'ān:

﴿إِنِّي وَجَّهْتُ وَجْهِيَ لِلَّذِي فَطَرَ ٱلسَّمَٰوَٰتِ وَٱلْأَرْضَ حَنِيفًاۖ وَمَآ أَنَا۠ مِنَ ٱلْمُشْرِكِينَ﴾

*﴾innī wajjahtu wajhiya li-lladhī faṭara s-samāwāti wa-l-'arḍa ḥanīfan wa-mā ana mina l-mushrikīn*[a]*﴿*

[50] Majlisī, ʿAllāmah Muḥammad Bāqir, *Biḥār al-Anwār*, Vol. 67, p. 25.

*﴾Indeed I have turned my face toward Him who originated the heavens and the earth, as a Hanif, and I am not one of the polytheists﴿*[51]

And the 'face' referred to in this verse is not simply the anatomical face. The worshipper must have an inner face with which he turns towards God ﷻ. If one does not have this inner face that has its own inner senses, how should one witness the beauty and magnificence of the Almighty Creator?

The worshipper turns with his body towards the qiblah, but there is another qiblah in this very world, which is a centre for Godly manifestations, and that is the heart of the believer. The believer's heart is described in this qudsī narration (narrated by the Holy Prophet ﷺ from God ﷻ):

> Neither can My skies contain Me, nor can My earth, but the heart of My faithful servant can contain Me.[52]

The praying person can look towards his own heart and be distracted by what he sees from anything else in this world.

---

[51] Sūrat al-An'ām, Verse 79.

[52] al-Aḥsā'ī, Ibn Abī Jumhūr, *'Awālī al-La'ālī al-'Azīziyyah fī al-Aḥādīth ad-Dīniyyah*, Vol. 4, p. 7.

# The Inner Etiquettes of the Prayer Time

He who claims to love God ﷻ should monitor himself when there is a conflict of interests, and something that reveals one's priorities is prayer at the beginning of its time. Whoever finds his wife or children closer to his heart than prayer in such times should know that there is an error in his priorities, even if he claims the contrary. God ﷻ has warned us in the Noble Qur'ān not to become distracted by possessions and family from His remembrance, when He said:

﴿لَا تُلْهِكُمْ أَمْوَالُكُمْ وَلَآ أَوْلَـٰدُكُمْ عَن ذِكْرِ ٱللَّهِ﴾

*﴿lā tulhikum amwālukum wa-lā awlādukum ʿan dhikri llāhi﴾*

*﴿Do not let your possessions and children distract you from the remembrance of God﴾*[53]

It is possible to say that the Holy verse

﴿ٱلَّذِينَ هُمْ عَن صَلَاتِهِمْ سَاهُونَ﴾

*﴿alladhīna hum ʿan ṣalātihim sāhūna﴾*

*﴿but are heedless of their prayers﴾*[54]

[53] Sūrat al-Munāfiqūn, Verse 9.

[54] Sūrat al-Māʿūn, Verse 5.

Applies to the person whose prayers are not accepted. To explain the verse, it has been said:

> That is: negligent and unconcerned about it (prayer), uncaring if they miss it completely, occasionally, or if they postpone it past its recommended time, and so on.[55]

It can also be said that being heedless includes delaying it without any excuse, as mentioned in the well-known narration from Imām Ja'far aṣ-Ṣādiq ﷺ, while commenting on the [above] honorable verse:

> Delaying the Ṣalāt from the beginning of its timing without an excuse.[56]

One who does not wake up for the Fajr prayer does not reap the benefits of the prayer that can change one's being. Prayer is like medication; it must be taken periodically and continuously, otherwise its effects are lost. There is a long gap between 'Ishā' and Ẓuhr prayers, and if a person does not pray Fajr, this long gap can harm their soul. How then does he expect to be a successful worshipper?!

---

[55] Ṭabāṭabā'ī, 'Allāmah Sayyid Muḥammad Ḥusayn, *al-Mīzān fī Tafsīr al-Qur'ān*, Vol. 20, p. 368.

[56] al-Ḥurr al-'Āmilī, Shaykh Muḥammad, *Wasā'il al-Shī'ah*, Vol. 4, p. 124.

God ﷻ, for reasons that remain known only to Him, gave some places and times a special superiority that distinguishes them from all others; the four mosques in which the worshipper is allowed to choose between praying Qaṣr or Tamaam being an example of such places, and the stations of distinction in the three months of worship (Rajab, Shaʿbān, and Ramaḍān) being an example of such times. Amongst the times that have their own exclusivity are prayer times, during which the doors to the heavens are opened, and the servant's efforts in closing the gap between himself and his Lord are more likely to be rewarded. It is narrated that Imām Jaʿfar aṣ-Ṣādiq ؑ said:

> The outstanding quality of the beginning of the time for prayer is like the outstanding quality of the next life compared to the worldly life.[57]

Divine Attention is available throughout the prayer. Still, the farther the worshipper is from the beginning of time, the farther away he finds himself from that exclusive Divine Attention. For this reason it is said that there is in prayer at the start of the time God's satisfaction, and the end of the time His forgiveness, as is narrated from Imām Jaʿfar aṣ-Ṣādiq ؑ:

[57] Kulaynī, Shaykh Muḥammad b. Yaʿqūb, *al-Kāfī*, Vol. 3, p. 274.

> The beginning of the time is the satisfaction of God, and the end of it is His forgiveness, and forgiveness does not occur except if there is a sin...[58]

God ﷻ could have tasked His servants with all of the rakʿahs of a day at one time. But instead, He wanted the worshipper to divide the prayer across several stations throughout his day, infusing his daily activity with the light of intermittent worship. This is the meaning of 'persevering' in the Holy Verse:

﴿الَّذِينَ هُمْ عَلَىٰ صَلَاتِهِمْ دَائِمُونَ﴾

*﴾alladhīna hum ʿalā ṣalātihim dāʾimūna﴿*

*﴾those who persevere in their prayers﴿*[59]

and the meaning of 'watchful' in:

﴿وَالَّذِينَ هُمْ عَلَىٰ صَلَاتِهِمْ يُحَافِظُونَ﴾

*﴾wa-lladhīna hum ʿalā ṣalātihim yuḥāfiẓūna﴿*

*﴾and those who are watchful of their prayers﴿*[60]

---

[58] al-Ḥurr al-ʿĀmilī, Shaykh Muḥammad, *Wasāʾil al-Shīʿah*, Vol. 4, p. 123.

[59] Sūrat al-Maʿārij, Verse 23.

[60] Sūrat al-Maʿārij, Verse 34.

Some people may focus their worship on a few specific points during the day when they pray the obligatory daily prayers. But the sincere servants do not limit themselves to those times; rather, they fill the gaps between those checkpoints with dhikr and turning to God ﷻ, in fulfilment of the Holy Verse:

﴿وَٱذْكُر رَّبَّكَ إِذَا نَسِيتَ﴾

﴿*wa-dhkur rabbaka idhā nasīta*﴾

﴿*And when you forget, remember your Lord*﴾[61]

In this way, their entire day seems filled with worship and remembrance of God ﷻ.

If a person wishes to test his proximity to God ﷻ, he should observe his actions at the entry of prayer time; if he finds himself sluggish or even surprised by the prayer time, to the point where it seems he wishes it were later so he can finish what he is already busy with, then he should realise that this is a sign of his remoteness from God ﷻ. The true lover is distinguished in such times, where his excitement and enthusiasm to meet his Lord is more important than anything else, and he prepares for such a meeting even before the time of prayer.

---

[61] Sūrat al-Kahf, Verse 24.

Those seeking Kamaal and success must utilise the special times during the day and night when worship and deeds are regarded more highly than at other times. Such times include the period between Fajr and sunrise, for it is the time in which blessings are determined, and the few hours before the dawn call to prayer, which is a staple time in the lives of the firm believers, for it is the time in which God ﷻ presents Himself to them. Everybody who wishes to attain a praiseworthy position in life must have a meeting with his Lord in this blessed time.

One of the most important stations of worship is the 'Middle Prayer' mentioned in the Noble Qur'ān. Interpreters have debated its meaning for centuries, and perhaps it refers to the Ẓuhr prayer because it is performed during the busiest time of the day, when a person is completely distracted by the labour of life. The true believer at this time realises that he must stop his activity to stand in the presence of his Lord. It is narrated that the Prophet ﷺ said:

> When the sun passes noon, the gates of Heaven and Paradise open and the supplications are accepted. So, blessed is he whose good deeds are lifted at that.[62]

The person who concerns himself with the importance of sincere prayer even before the time for prayer has arrived is setting himself up for success in his prayers. This is through

---

[62] Ṣadūq, Shaykh Muḥammad b. 'Alī, *al-Amālī*, p. 575.

limiting the amount of worldly distracting matters first, then asking for God's assistance in fighting the devils hovering around his heart, waiting for the right opportunity to catch him in their traps. Shayṭān becomes greedier during the times in which the believer wants to move closer to God ﷻ, and what better time than at the time of prayer, the pillar of his entire religion? The narrations from the Holy Prophet ﷺ state that:

> He comes between a man and his self and says,
>
> Think of such and such, think of such and such,
>
> which he was not thinking about before, until the man does not know how much he has prayed.[63]

Some people try their absolute hardest to control their imagination during prayer, but to no avail, because the Devil's whispers interfere with their mind, distracting them and making the struggle unbearable. The secret is that this struggle is the mind's struggle, which, ultimately, is difficult to control. So what is the problem with involving the body in the matter? A person can condition himself to pray at the beginning of prayer time, whatever it takes, hoping that through this he can make up for the flaws in his heart. Over time, he gains the ability for his interior to match his exterior, and he can pray on time with sincerity of the

---

[63] *Sharḥ Furūʿ al-Kāfī*, Vol. 3, 256.

heart. In a narration from Imām Ja'far aṣ-Ṣādiq ﷷ, in which he explains the verse

﴿ٱلَّذِينَ هُمْ عَن صَلَاتِهِمْ سَاهُونَ﴾

﴿*alladhīna hum 'an ṣalātihim sāhūna*﴾

﴿*but are heedless of their prayers*﴾[64]

He ﷷ is asked:

> Is it the insinuation of Shayṭān?

He ﷷ said:

> No, everyone is hit by this insinuation. But it is being heedless of it, and leaving the prayer during the beginning of its time.[65]

Performing prayers at the beginning of their time consistently and in all cases in not always going to be easy, and will often require a great deal of effort and willpower; struggling to stand up in times of illness, or willing oneself out of a warm bed to perform tahajjud in the middle of the night, or tearing oneself from the commotions of life for Ẓuhr and 'Aṣr prayers. But know that the harder the

---

[64] Sūrat al-Mā'ūn, Verse 5.

[65] al-Ḥurr al-'Āmilī, Shaykh Muḥammad, *Wasā'il al-Shī'ah*, Vol. 4, p. 114.

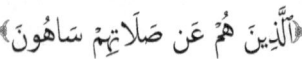

struggle, the faster the advance towards God ﷻ, as is narrated from Imām ʿAlī ؑ:

> The best act is that which you have to force yourself to do.[66]

One of the many blessings of performing prayers on time is that it transforms the servant into a disciplined being in all aspects of life. Performing one's duties at the specified times is a factor in success, not just in the afterlife, but also in this life. Additionally, fulfilling one's promises and duties on time is a sign of a true believer. Imām ʿAlī ؑ once gave some valuable advice by saying:

> I advise you and all my children and members of my family and everyone whom my writing reaches, to fear God, to keep your affairs in order.[67]

---

[66] Sharīf Raḍī, Muḥammad b. al-Ḥusayn, *Nahj al-Balāghah*, p. 511.

[67] Ibid., p. 421.

# The Inner Etiquettes of the Place of Prayer

Designating a specific place in one's home to stand between the hands of God ﷻ is an excellent way to foster focus and sincerity in one's worship. Sometimes the person may even find himself standing in that place, reminiscing about his earnestness, which in turn gives him the confidence to recreate that ambiance with some effort, accompanied by Tawassul. This is why we read in the Noble Qur'ān:

﴿كُلَّمَا دَخَلَ عَلَيْهَا زَكَرِيَّا ٱلْمِحْرَابَ وَجَدَ عِندَهَا رِزْقًا﴾

*﴾kullamā dakhala 'alayhā zakariyyā l-miḥrāba wajada 'indahā rizqan﴿*

*﴾Whenever Zechariah visited her in the sanctuary, he would find provisions with her﴿*[68]

We understand from this verse that Maryam عليها السلام reserved a special sanctuary in her abode where she could approach her Almighty Lord. Indeed, some worshippers go a step further, dedicating a specific garment they have carefully chosen and perfumed, and are certain it is clean and permissible to wear in prayer.

Prostrating upon the turbah of Imām al-Ḥusayn عليه السلام greatly influences the acceptance of one's prayer, as is narrated from Imām Ja'far aṣ-Ṣādiq عليه السلام:

---

68 Sūrat Āl 'Imrān, Verse 37.

> Prostrating on the turbah of Imām al-Ḥusayn illuminates all seven earths.[69]

It is also narrated that he ﷺ said:

> Our Shīʿah never abandon four: a tablet he prays upon, a ring he wears, a toothbrush he brushes his teeth with, and a rosary from clay of the grave of Imām al-Ḥusayn ﷺ.[70]

Undoubtedly, this great esteem stems solely from its connection to this great and pure individual who sacrificed everything he had for his beloved Master. From here, we understand that the path to excelling in the eyes of God ﷻ and earning the honor of associating with Him lies in tolerating some amount of suffering for the sake of God ﷻ, and beyond that lie rewards of unimaginable varieties!

It is mustaḥabb to move a dying person to his prayer area at the hour of his death, since being in that place in such an hour brings about God's mercy, and also provokes pity in the angels around him, including the Angel of Death. In fact, it is narrated that the believer's prayer area cries for him when he passes away, as mentioned in the narration from Imām ʿAlī ﷺ:

---

[69] al-Ḥurr al-ʿĀmilī, Shaykh Muḥammad, *Wasāʾil al-Shīʿah*, Vol. 5, p. 366.

[70] Ibid., p. 359.

> When the servant dies, his prayer place weeps for him from the Earth, and his ascended acts weep for him from the sky.[71]

Therefore, it is recommended that the servant reserve a spot in his house specifically for prayer, where he is isolated from all the distractions that fill our homes these days.

The first stage of ṭahārah required in prayer is the ṭahārah of the location, followed by the ṭahārah of the attire, then the ṭahārah of the body. However, we must also focus on the cleanliness of the closest thing to the human being, which is none other than his soul. But how many of us spend so much time obsessing over the three aforementioned stages of ṭahārah, and completely forget about the fourth stage, upon which the prayer's acceptance relies the most?

---

[71] Ghazzālī, Abū Ḥamīd, *Iḥyā' 'Ulūm ad-Dīn*, Vol. 1, p. 152.

# The Inner Etiquettes of the Adhān and Iqāmah

There is a strong resemblance between the parts of the adhān and iqāmah: both start with takbīr and end with tahlīl. They both also mention the Holy Prophet ﷺ, and so both the Mu'adhdhin and the worshipper allude to the concepts of Tawḥīd and Nubuwwah in every prayer. And these two things—that is, paying Attention to the station of the Lord and mentioning the message of His Prophet and his servitude to Him—are recurring elements in and throughout all prayers, as we see in adhān, iqāmah, rukūʿ, sujūd, tashahhud, and taslīm.

In a beautiful picture of Divine repayment to His faithful servants, God ﷻ immortalised the name of His Holy Prophet ﷺ in the adhān and iqāmah, tashahhud and taslīm, rukūʿ and sujūd, even going as far as praying upon him at all times. God ﷻ and His angels pray upon the Holy Prophet ﷺ constantly and infinitely, as is indicated by the present tense verb, indicating continuity, in the Holy Verse:

﴿إِنَّ ٱللَّهَ وَمَلَٰٓئِكَتَهُۥ يُصَلُّونَ عَلَى ٱلنَّبِيِّ يَٰٓأَيُّهَا ٱلَّذِينَ ءَامَنُواْ صَلُّواْ عَلَيۡهِ وَسَلِّمُواْ تَسۡلِيمًا﴾

*﴿inna llāha wa-malā'ikatahū yuṣallūna ʿalā n-nabiyyi yā-'ayyuhā lladhīna āmanū ṣallū ʿalayhi wa-sallimū taslīma$^{n}$﴾*

*﴾Undeed God and His angels bless the Prophet; O you who have faith! Invoke blessings on him and invoke Peace upon him in a worthy manner﴿*[72]

The meaning of the declaration "Qad qāmat aṣ-Ṣalāh (prayer has been established)" is an invitation for the servant to not only perform prayer, but to establish it too. And performing prayer is something different from establishing and maintaining it. The Noble Qur'ān has confirmed this fact in all verses calling to prayer, for there is not a single instance in which the Qur'ān tells us to 'pray', 'perform prayer', or 'complete the prayer'. We are always told to maintain the prayer, such as in the Holy Verse:

﴿أَقِمِ ٱلصَّلَوٰةَ لِدُلُوكِ ٱلشَّمْسِ إِلَىٰ غَسَقِ ٱلَّيْلِ وَقُرْءَانَ ٱلْفَجْرِ إِنَّ قُرْءَانَ ٱلْفَجْرِ كَانَ مَشْهُودًا﴾

*﴾aqimi ṣ-ṣalāta li-dulūki sh-shamsi ilā ghasaqi l-layli﴿*

*﴾Maintain the prayer [during the period] from the sun's decline till the darkness of the night﴿*[73]

The idea of 'establishing prayer' is similar to the example of erecting a tent, as explained in the narration from the Holy Prophet ﷺ:

---

[72] Sūrat al-Aḥzāb, Verse 56.

[73] Sūrat al-Isrā', Verse 78.

> Prayer is like the pole of a tent. If the pole is established, then the ropes, pegs, and covering are all beneficial, but if the pole breaks, none of the ropes, pegs, or covering work.[74]

Between the adhān and iqāmah exists a good opportunity for the servant to contemplate and reflect through lowering himself to the ground and prostrating before his Lord. This is a tradition we have learnt from our Imāms عليهم السلام, for it is narrated from Imām Jaʿfar aṣ-Ṣādiq عليه السلام that:

> Amīr al-Mu'minīn, Imām ʿAlī b. Abī Ṭālib, used to say to his companions:
>
> > One who prostrates between the adhān and the iqāmah, and says in his sajdah:
> >
> > > Lord! I prostrate to You, fearfully, humbly!
> >
> > God the Exalted Says:
> >
> > > My Angels! By My might and My majesty! I shall instil love of him in the hearts of My faithful servants, and awe of him in the hearts of the hypocrites![75]

---

[74] Kulaynī, Shaykh Muḥammad b. Yaʿqūb, *al-Kāfī*, Vol. 3, p. 266.

[75] al-Ḥurr al-ʿĀmilī, Shaykh Muḥammad, *Wasāʾil al-Shīʿah*, Vol. 5, p. 400.

In this beautiful act of servitude, the most dignified place on the servant's face, being the forehead, is placed on the shoddiest material in existence, being dirt. There is no doubt that this act accelerates the servant's ascension to his Lord tenfold, on the condition that it is performed with Attention and deliberation, not just as a simple bodily motion.

When a person goes to make ziyārah to a Maʿṣūm, it is mustaḥabb for him to seek permission before entering the Holy Shrine, and he should not enter the sanctuary without shedding a single tear, even if minuscule, as if this tenderness were a sign of permission to enter. And it is possible to achieve this during prayer. What prohibits the worshipper to say between him and himself:

> Oh Lord! I want to make takbīr to enter the prayer. Do you allow me to pray in your presence and seek your sanctuary?!

And how fortunate is the one to have his tears flow in such a position, raising his hands for takbīr; a takbīr that has the potential to rip through the seven skies and reach His Almighty Presence. Truly, the sight of a servant weeping before the Almighty and Powerful Lord is among the greatest scenes in the realm of existence.

If one approaches prayer after the bustle of life and its various exchanges and interactions, their heart would be like murky water. In this case, he must wait a little while before trying to connect with his Lord, to decontaminate his heart and gather his thoughts. Here comes the role of the adhān and iqāmah in restoring balance to the worshipper, given that they are performed with deliberation and awareness of their inter-dimensional values. This is especially important, considering Shayṭān's readiness to pounce on any insecurities the worshipper has during Prayer, which is why we see that a worshipper can sometimes be clear-headed and ready for Prayer. Still, the moment he enters Prayer, he is overwhelmed by worries and distractions.

The servant reiterates his prayers five times a day, every day for his entire life. This sort of repetition can cause him to overlook the deeper values of prayer due to its monotony, and he ends up just repeating phrases he does not truly understand. This is because his nervous system is getting used to the tongue's routine movements. Hence, the servant must put in some extra effort to comprehend what is being said during the adhān and iqāmah, considering they are the opening phrases of every prayer, then complete his mental and spiritual preparation before standing up for takbir, so that he enters prayer with total preparation to meet his Gracious Lord.

One of the major obstacles to prayer is that it carries serious consequences if not done sincerely by the worshipper, as he would be a liar deserving punishment and rebuke for his hypocrisy. An example of this is the opening of the adhān. It starts with takbīr (God is greater), which means that

God ﷻ is greater than any description we may give Him, an understanding of which instils humility in the person. Similarly, the adhān concludes with tahlīl (there is no God but God), from which we understand that there is no deity deserving worship. Still, God ﷻ, and this meaning can be inferred in the narration of Imām Jaʿfar aṣ-Ṣādiq ؑ:

> And condition your heart to glorify Him upon hearing takbīr, and despise the material world and what is in it, to not be dishonest in your takbir. And reject in your heart any deity except Him upon hearing tahlīl.[76]

The adhān and iqāmah are essentially an invitation from God ﷻ to His servants to present themselves before Him, for they were revealed to the Holy Prophet ﷺ as jurisdiction from our Almighty Lord Himself. Thus, it is only appropriate that we contemplate its phrases, and ponder over how God ﷻ calls us to prayer twenty times a day, and to success and the greatest of worships the same number of times. He then commanded the establishment of the prayer ten times, raising the total number of calls to prayer to seventy. In other words, throughout the five adhāns every day, God beckons us to His Presence seventy times, so imagine the sheer insolence of the person who ignores this repeated summoning, and the distance between him and his Lord, especially if he was being distracted by the most trivial and petty of matters!

---

[76] Narāqī, Muḥaqqiq, *Jāmiʿ al-Saʿādāt*, Vol. 3, p. 271.

# The Inner Etiquettes of Intention

Upon reaching the stage of the niyyah, he who truly wants to feel the humility of standing before his Almighty Lord must sense that fear of failure and rejection, according to what the Qur'ān says when describing charitable people:

﴿وَٱلَّذِينَ يُؤْتُونَ مَآ ءَاتَوا۟ وَّقُلُوبُهُمْ وَجِلَةٌ﴾

*﴿wa-lladhīna yu'tūna mā ātaw wa-qulūbuhum wajilatun﴾*

*﴿who give whatever they give while their hearts tremble with awe﴾*[77]

A state caused by the fear of rejection. And so the true believer, upon reaching the niyyah before takbīr, experiences this uncertainty and anxiety, which in turn prepares the worshipper for a sincere prayer from its first component, which is the niyyah. At this phase, just before takbir, it is more appropriate for the worshipper to prepare himself mentally and revise his intention of Qurbah, instead of obsessing over things to say, to undergo the true aura of niyyah.

Love in the realm of the Divine differs completely from love in our world, a world in which the love diminishes when the two lovers finally meet, whereas there is no diminishing of Divine love. Rather, it surges and swells

---

[77] Sūrat al-Mu'minūn, Verse 60.

upon meeting the Creator. In fact, there is another law in that blessed realm; there is no repetition in the meetings. And witness to this is what sincere worshippers experience, as every heartfelt prayer differs from the other. And the reason for this is that God ﷻ looks at His servant differently at every moment. It is narrated that the Prophet ﷺ said:

> God ﷻ approaches the servant during his prayer as long as the servant does not turn away. If the servant turns away his face, God ﷻ turns away from him.[78]

One of the signs of a pure niyyah is that the person's state in secret is identical to his state in public. For this reason, the servants who consistently pray Ṣalāt al-Layl are safe from riyā' in their prayers during the day, because they have successfully passed the test of genuineness. So when the soul comes to taunt him during his prayer in public—by shaming him for riyā', for example—he repels it by saying

> Don't prevent me from my earnestness in public,
> for I have been earnest with my Lord in secret.

This is one of the blessings of hidden worship, in that the worshipper does not care about those around him in open worship.

We can expand our exclusive and limited niyyah in our prayer, and make it encompass all the other aspects of our

[78] al-Ḥakim al-Nīshābūrī, *al-Mustadrak 'ala al-Ṣaḥīḥayn*, Vol. 1, p. 504.

lives. In other words, the clever servant can intend all his daily toils and activities to be in the service of God ﷻ, even going as far as to wish that his death may be in the service of his Lord, so he may be truly triumphant in his life, as is depicted in the Holy Verse:

﴿قُلْ إِنَّ صَلَاتِي وَنُسُكِي وَمَحْيَايَ وَمَمَاتِي لِلَّهِ رَبِّ ٱلْعَٰلَمِينَ﴾

*﴾qul inna ṣalātī wa-nusukī wa-maḥyāya wa-mamātī li-llāhi rabbi l-ʿālamīna*[a]*﴿*

*﴾Say, 'Indeed my prayer and my worship, my life and my death are for the sake of God, the Lord of all the worlds'﴿*[79]

It is possible for a believer to reach a stage at which he sees no beauty other than the beauty of his Almighty Lord, and every other beautiful thing he may see in this world, whether human or natural beauty, only points him towards his Lord. Should one want to witness the majesty and beauty of God ﷻ in full on the Day of Judgement, he should grasp the ability to see it in this world first.

It is not a secret that whoever spends enough time performing prayers sincerely will begin to notice a certain exquisiteness in his worship. An exquisiteness that overtakes any other beautiful thing he has seen in his life. After witnessing such extreme beauty, does one really need to put in that much effort to be sincere in their prayer?

---

[79] Sūrat al-Anʿām, Verse 162.

It is essential to differentiate between trivial whispers that pass through the heart during prayer and those that remain in the heart, influencing the person whenever he wants to perform a good deed. Here, careful self-observation is crucial. If one fears that riyāʾ influences their prayer but notices that their prayer in public is identical to their prayer in private, they should know that it is none other than Shayṭān manipulating them to remove all sincerity from their prayers.

Mustering the strength of the soul at the stage of the niyyah is necessary to reach the state of eagerness for prayer. Naturally, gathering the stray fragments of the soul after they have been scattered throughout the day is not an easy task, and it takes immense effort to wrap them all up together and carry them toward His Almighty presence. And perhaps now is a good opportunity to mention what the great scholar, Sayyid Yazdī, mentions in his book:

> Correctness and completion differ from acceptance, for an act of worship may be correct in a way that its performer is not considered negligent, nor does he deserve punishment, but it remains unsatisfactory to the Lord. The main condition of acceptance is the desire of the heart for worship, for it is his soul, and it is just like the body. If the desire is present during the entire prayer, it is entirely accepted, and if not, it is accepted by the proportion it was present. Hence, half

> the prayer may be accepted, or a third of it, or a quarter, and so on...[80]

Just as we must be cautious of riyāʾ, which comes with a deed, we must also be very careful of ʿujb, which comes after it, as it is also an obstacle to the acceptance of a deed. This is quite common in those who experience a heartfelt prayer once as a coincidence, as opposed to the sincere servants who are accustomed to such prayers, and therefore are immune to these corruptions, like riyāʾ, ʿujb, and intrusions. And since we are talking about obstacles to acceptance, let us list a few things that have been cited as impediments: delaying zakāt and other obligatory duties; envy, arrogance, and backbiting; consuming ḥarām foods and alcohol. It has even been narrated that Imām Jaʿfar aṣ-Ṣādiq عليه السلام said:

> If one looks with anger at his parents, even when they are unjust to him, God will not accept any of his prayers.[81]

A servant may perform his prayer in such a way that means it is accepted, but does things that deny him a lot of its blessings, such as approaching it with extreme sluggishness and sleepiness, or being distracted in it, or rushing it, or praying while needing to use the restroom, or letting his

---

[80] al-Yazdī, Sayyid Muḥammad Kāẓim, *al-ʿUrwat al-Wuthqā*, Vol. 1, p. 612.

[81] Kulaynī, Shaykh Muḥammad b. Yaʿqūb, *al-Kāfī*, Vol. 2, p. 349.

sight drift up towards the ceiling. Rather, one must try to perform actions that increase one's reward and status, such as using perfume, wearing clean clothes, wearing a carnelian (ʿaqīq/agate) ring, combing the hair, brushing the teeth, etc.

# The Inner Etiquettes of Takbīr

The six opening takbīrs—done before the obligatory one—are a good opportunity for one to gradually wade into the sea of prayer before his Lord after perfecting his niyyah. And perfecting niyyah only comes with bringing about prayer's true essence, which can be summarised into: the intention of obeying the Divine orders, and not thinking of anything else during it; not even the rewards in the hereafter; not even one's proximity to his Lord.

The most recurring phrase in prayer is takbīr (God is Great), the true meaning of which is the inability to accurately describe God ﷻ, for this speechlessness is the ultimate description. It is narrated that a man once said 'Allāhu Akbar' in front of Imām Ja'far aṣ-Ṣādiq ؑ, to which the Imām said:

> God is greater than what thing?

The man replied,

> Greater than everything.

Abū 'Abd Allāh ؑ said,

> You have limited Him.

The man asked,

> Then, how should I say it?

He replied,

Say,

God is greater than what can be described[82]

The physical movements considered mustaḥabb during prayer signify reverence for God ﷻ, as the servant gives a portion of the prayer for his body to perform. Thus, it is sensible for the worshipper to look into the specified actions in prayer, whether wājib or mustaḥabb, to make sure that his movements correlate with what God ﷻ wants from him. An example of this is the mustaḥabb movement during takbīr, where the worshipper raises his hands, fingers together, palms facing the qiblah as he says the takbīr. This begins when he starts raising his hands and is completed by the time his hands are beside his neck.

Just as we seek help from the Infallible Imāms عليهم السلام in fulfilling our worldly desires, what stops us from asking them for help in spiritual needs, such as a sincere prayer, the reward for which is all goodness? It is narrated that Imām ʿAlī ar-Riḍā عليه السلام said:

> One should say after proclaiming the iqāmah and before beginning prayer, during every prayer:
>
> > O God, Lord of this complete supplication and the prayer being established! Provide Muḥammad the rank, and the means, and the grace, and the merit. I

[82] Kulaynī, Shaykh Muḥammad b. Yaʿqūb, *al-Kāfī*, Vol. 1, p. 117.

begin with God, and with God I succeed, and by Muḥammad, the Prophet of God, and his Progeny, I orient myself! Make me through them, in Your presence, worthy of regard in the world and the hereafter, and among those of proximity.[83]

This all-important prayer is as similar as possible to a paramount exam, and the exam hall is the mosque. We all know how it feels to approach a life-changing exam, anxious and in a state of total focus and concentration! Similarly, one must scrutinise the self closely when approaching prayer, instructing it at takbīr, monitoring it during the prayer, and assessing it after taʿqīb, punishing it if he sees any flaw in his prayer. Reasonable punishments include praying some mustaḥabb prayers in the mosque after his daily prayers, such as the prayer of Jaʿfar or the prayer of al-Ḥujjah عليه السلام, to regain the esteem he lost for not praying sincerely. This concept of punishment is an excellent motivator to make extra effort during prayer to achieve that invaluable mental concentration.

We must accustom ourselves to venerate the Name of God عز وجل. Not just when it is written, but even when it is spoken. We pronounce God's Name and pronouns referring to Him multiple times in prayer. Therefore, just as we say ṣalawāt for the Holy Prophet ﷺ when we mention his name, or send our salāmāt to the Imāms عليهم السلام when saying

---

83 Ṭūsī, Shaykh Muḥammad b. Ḥasan, *Miṣbāḥ al-Mutahajjid wa Silāḥ al-Mutaʿabbid*, Vol. 1, p. 72.

their names, we should also make sure to include words of respect to God ﷻ when uttering His Name outside of prayer, rather than just saying His Name unadorned with any expressions of glorification.

Takbīrat al-Iḥrām is comparable to an official entry into the sanctuary of meeting God ﷻ. Before uttering the takbīr, it is like a person is standing before closed doors, awaiting his meeting with a great emperor, and just by pronouncing the takbīr, he is escorted into the courtyard in which he is to meet this emperor, along with all that it entails, including the things that void the prayer. Hence, if the servant enters the court of the emperor with respect and reverence, he is expected to continue with his respect and may be forgiven for some amount of disrespect that slips out of him. Alternatively, if the person is disrespectful from the first moment of the encounter, he will be considered insolent, even if he behaves appropriately later.

Takbīrat al-Iḥrām is one of the factors that makes the worshipper truly feel the weight of responsibility on his shoulder. When he recites Sūrat al-Fātiḥah and another Sūrah, then bows and prostrates, he must realise that he stands before One who is greater than any description can fit appropriately. It is as if this takbīr serves as an incentive for the worshipper to perfect his prayer. So it is understandable that the servant's prayer may be filled with intermittent takbirs at every step, as he starts his prayer with Takbīrat al-Iḥrām, then says takbir before rukūʿ and after it, then before sujūd and after, until he ends his prayer with three mustaḥabb takbīrs. And so he is constantly living in the aura of the takbir, which reminds him of his oath to his Almighty Lord at the beginning of his prayer in his Takbīrat al-Iḥrām.

One who does not hold any reverence for his Creator in his eyes leaves a crater in his soul that he naturally fills with things other than God ﷻ. Hence, the worship of true believers is seamless and natural, with their prayers flowing into movements that correspond to their emotions. The Qur'ān says:

﴿وَٱسْتَعِينُوا۟ بِٱلصَّبْرِ وَٱلصَّلَوٰةِ ۚ وَإِنَّهَا لَكَبِيرَةٌ إِلَّا عَلَى ٱلْخَٰشِعِينَ﴾

﴾*wa-sta'īnū bi-ṣ-ṣabri wa-ṣ-ṣalāti wa-'innahā la-kabīratun illā 'alā l-khāshi'īn*[a]﴿

﴾*And take recourse in patience and prayer, and it is indeed hard except for the humble*﴿[84]

In fact, they even complain that they are unable to admire anyone but God ﷻ, as that requires a void in their souls. Still, that void does not exist because the true believer is he who sees no catalyst in this world except their Almighty Lord.

God's ﷻ faithful worshippers adore prayer and enjoy praising God ﷻ so much so that they forget their physical

[84] Sūrat al-Baqarah, Verse 45.

form at takbīr, as they are overcome with the flooding of emotions in their hearts. We see how Amīr al-Mu'minīn ﷺ would have arrows removed from his body during prayer, and he would feel nothing. Some sincere worshippers would resemble dry wood during prayer as a result of their total immersion in the superior realms. And it is no wonder, since we read in the Noble Qur'ān that:

﴿فَلَمَّا رَأَيْنَهُۥٓ أَكْبَرْنَهُۥ وَقَطَّعْنَ أَيْدِيَهُنَّ﴾

*﴿fa-lammā ra'aynahū akbarnahū wa-qaṭṭa'na aydiyahunna﴾*

*﴿So when they saw him, they marvelled at him and cut their hands [absent-mindedly]﴾*[85]

for they have seen the beauty of Prophet Yūsuf ﷺ, which is but a human finite beauty. Imagine Amīr al-Mu'minīn's ﷺ state when witnessing the beauty of his Divine Lord! Is his infatuation with such beauty even comparable to the infatuation of those women?!

The sincere worshipper is he who pays full Attention right from the beginning of the prayer, when he recites Takbīrat al-Iḥrām, to protect himself from doubts and uncertainties, which are a sign that the servant is not fully attentive to his Lord. These doubts, such as whether one is currently in a rak'ah, though they have clear jurisprudential solutions, are

[85] Sūrat Yūsuf, Verse 31.

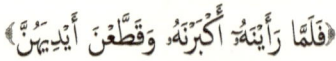

something true believers find intolerable. It is unacceptable for a sincere worshipper to find himself in such uncertainty and neglect! Therefore, it is crucial to put more effort and focus from the moment he says his takbīr, to keep his prayer under a watchful eye from its opening, and not to be gradually dragged into the state of forgetfulness and obliviousness that causes such doubts.

The servant begins his prayer with Takbīrat al-ihram, claiming that God ﷻ is greater than can be described, which denotes sensing the glory of God ﷻ and ignoring anything else. Hence, turning away from God immediately after the takbīr means that this prayer is initiated with a false claim. How can a servant be accepted if he commences it with a clear contradiction?! Furthermore, this contradiction recurs with every subsequent takbīr, as well as when he says:

﴿إِيَّاكَ نَعْبُدُ وَإِيَّاكَ نَسْتَعِينُ﴾

*﴿iyyāka na'budu wa-'iyyāka nasta'īnu﴾*

*﴿You [alone] do we worship, and to You [alone] do we turn for help﴾*[86]

When he is very clearly turning to others! So the worshipper must be at least somewhat honest, meaning he should be truthful in his initial claim, glorifying God

[86] Sūrat al-Fātiḥah, Verse 5.

during the takbīr, even if he is incapable of being devout in the later stages of prayer.

# The Inner Mysteries of Seeking Refuge (Istiʿādhah)

It is mustaḥabb for one to recite istiʿādhah, asking God ﷻ for protection against the whispers of Shayṭān, before commencing recitation in prayer, because Shayṭān wishes to spoil any form of worship that the servant performs, internally and externally. If he is unable to void it completely from the outside, he will work on corrupting it from the inside. Shayṭān has a deep grudge against human beings, which leads him to work hard to distract the servant from performing acts of worship as God ﷻ wants them performed.

Some internal actions have mistakenly been restricted to words alone, such as istiʿādhah and istighfār, which are meant to be performed by the heart, even when expressed with the tongue. So when a person asks God ﷻ for forgiveness, he repents primarily with his heart, and when he asks for God's mercy, his heart seeks refuge in Him first. So these spoken words were meant to signify internal emotions; hence, if the heart is void of these emotions, the words do not affect the heart as they are meant to.

When the worshipper seeks refuge in God ﷻ from Shayṭān through istiʿādhah must not forget that this initial istiʿādhah not exempt him of continuous istiʿādhah. Just like the niyyah, istiʿādhah must be continuous in the prayer from its beginning to its end, because maybe Shayṭān is waiting for him in a later stage of the prayer, like during rukūʿ or 'ujood, which is why we see that a worshipper can be devoted in the beginning of the prayer, but lose his earnestness in the middle or end of it.

Shayṭān exploits a person's internal insecurities to sidetrack him during prayer. And so the servant must see through these tricks by restraining his emotions, controlling them instead of letting them control him. There is no harm in thoughts that pass the mind arbitrarily, as they are involuntary, and God ﷻ is greater than to punish His servant for something which was not by choice. The real problem lies in following those thoughts voluntarily and letting them take over the mind. These thoughts come like the end of a string, and if the person grabs onto that string, Shayṭān drags him wherever he likes. So the liability and culpability are not based on the original thought, but on allowing that thought to develop.

It is peculiar that the onslaught of mental distractions increases during prayer. A worshipper may be at an acceptable level of concentration before prayer, an acceptable level of internal commitment. Still, the instant he raises his hands for Takbīrat al-Iḥrām, he is flooded with various emotions and disturbances, almost as if a hand is pulling him away from performing his duty appropriately, distracting him from the condition of being before his Lord. This is attested to by the narration of the Holy Prophet ﷺ:

> When any one of you stands for prayer, Shayṭān comes and puts him in doubt till he forgets how many rakʿāt he prayed.[87]

And it is known that controlling these disturbances, whether outside of prayer or during it, is very challenging for those not accustomed to sincere and heartfelt prayers. This is because concentration on something originates from that thing's essence in the heart. So the person who does not hold for his Lord any regard in his heart will naturally be denied focusing on Him during prayer.

Simply uttering verbal phrases that the heart does not correspond to is not only futile, but it can even be said that it does the worshipper more harm than good, as the devils around him strike back at him, for he has just tried to break free from their control and join the ranks of sincere worshippers. So the devils double their efforts to retaliate against this effort and prevent any further attempts. The true believer, on the other hand, seeks refuge in God's ﷻ fortress, which is the fortress of Tawḥīd as depicted in His saying

> Lā ilāha illā Allāh is my fortress.[88]

And the fort of wilāyah, as it is also narrated that

---

[87] Bukhārī, Muḥammad b. Ismāʿīl, *Ṣaḥīḥ Bukhārī*, Vol. 2, p. 69.

[88] Ṣadūq, Shaykh Muḥammad b. ʿAlī, *al-Amālī*, p. 235.

Wilāyat 'Alī b. Abī Ṭālib is My fortress.[89]

[89] Majlisī, 'Allāmah Muḥammad Bāqir, *Biḥār al-Anwār*, Vol. 39, p. 246.

# The Inner Etiquettes of the Bismillāh

If there had been a greater expression than the Bismillāh (*Bi-smi llāhi r-Raḥmāni r-Raḥīm*), then God ﷻ would have used that expression in the openings of the Chapters of the Noble Qur'ān. This is why it is the most recurring verse in the Noble Qur'ān, and why it is customary for a speaker to start his speech with the Bismillāh and for an author to start his book with it, as no title is a more reflective mirror than the Bismillāh. And it should be known that, contrary to some beliefs, the Bismillāh is an integral part of all the Chapters of the Noble Qur'ān, except Sūrat at-Tawbah, and serious reprimanding has been reported to be aimed at those who omit it, such as the narration from Imām Ja'far aṣ-Ṣādiq ؑ:

> What is the matter with them? May God contest them! They are confronting the mightiest Verse in the Book of God, and they are claiming that it is a transgression if they were to recite it, and it is: In the Name of God, the Beneficent, the Merciful.[90]

Reciting Bismillāh is like taking permission from the owner of an object to use said object. And that is a common form of respect and decorum between people: if someone wants to take something from someone else, they ask for their permission first, even if they already know the other person does not mind. Similarly, a dedicated servant sees himself constantly under the watchful gaze of his Lord, so if he

---

[90] Majlisī, 'Allāmah Muḥammad Bāqir, *Biḥār al-Anwār*, Vol. 82, p. 21.

wants to utilise something his Lord has equipped him with, it is courteous for him to ask for his Lord's permission first. And taking permission from God ﷻ does not even require speech. All it needs is the privilege to be able to recite the Bismillāh, for God ﷻ is kinder and greater than to refuse permission to His servant after His servant glorifies Him! After all, what use is granting something to His servant if He does not permit him to use it, especially when He owns everything in existence?!

One of the blessings of Bismillāh is the preservation of any act. We see this clearly when the servant asks God through the Bismillāh for permission to do something, such as eating or drinking. Even if such an act actually derives from pure instinct, the servant tries to tie this action to the will of his Lord, even through indoctrination, so that it is as if God ﷻ Himself wants him to eat or drink for another, greater purpose: gaining strength for worship. By doing this, the servant has made his eating and drinking a form of worship for which he deserves a lofty reward! What a trade it is, to eat and drink from this finite sustenance, in return for an infinite reward!

The sentence *In the Name of God, the Beneficent, the Merciful* is an incomplete sentence that needs a subject, and that subject is the action that is commenced with the Bismillāh. And so this action can be related to a word or phrase, conceived as a subject. So it is as if he says: "I eat", or "I read", or "I perform this particular action" in the Name of God ﷻ. And, undoubtedly, any action commenced with the Name of God ﷻ is linked to Him. On the other hand, we find the narration from the Holy Prophet ﷺ that says:

> Every conscious act upon which God's name is not mentioned is futile.[91]

And to be without posterity means to be severed, with no legacy or remnant.

Another valuable blessing of the Bismillāh is its ability to prevent the worshipper from sinning. When the servant recites the Bismillāh, fully aware of its values, before performing an act of worship, he must ensure God's ﷻ approval of that act. He must make sure not to disobey God ﷻ in the beginning of it, nor to act against His will in the middle of it, for how can he claim that his act is linked to God ﷻ, which is the implication of Bismillāh, and ask for His blessings in it, and then disobey Him during that same act?! Indeed, he must have shame before his Lord if he even thinks about going against His will, because to recite Bismillāh before something implies using that thing for what pleases Him.

One of the effects of the Bismillāh is the prevention of the devils from breaching the boundaries of the act upon which the servant recited the Bismillāh, because the moment they hear God's ﷻ name, they shrink and

[91] al-Ḥurr al-ʿĀmilī, Shaykh Muḥammad, *Wasāʾil al-Shīʿah*, Vol. 7, p. 170.

withdraw, for fear of entering the dominion of God ﷻ. His dominion contains His faithful servants, about whom God ﷻ has said:

﴿إِنَّ عِبَادِي لَيْسَ لَكَ عَلَيْهِمْ سُلْطَانٌ﴾

*﴾inna 'ibādī laysa laka 'alayhim sulṭānun﴿*

*﴾As for My servants, you shall have no authority over them﴿*[92]

Thus, reciting the Bismillāh before an act ensures God's ﷻ blessings on the one hand, and thwarts Shayṭān's attempts to spoil it on the other, as God ﷻ has guaranteed. And so when the servant recites Bismillāh to recite Sūrat al-Fātiḥah, he is in fact invoking the request for permission to pray, the niyyah of repelling the devils,, and the niyyah to gain God's ﷻ mercy, which he expects to be rewarded with during his journey through the sea of prayer.

God ﷻ chose two of His Blessed Names, in addition to "God", to include in the Bismillāh, both of which contain the meaning of 'mercy', even though He could have used a variety of Names, like using "the Avenger" and "the Merciful" together to create a balance of fear and hope. However, it should be noted that 'mercy' has two connotations: the universal mercy that is bestowed on everything, and a special mercy reserved for the faithful. A

92 Sūrat al-Isrā', Verse 65.

case of this special mercy is that God ﷻ draws near His servant during prayer. Another example is the special relationship between the servant and his Lord, even outside prayer, as described in the narration from Imām Jaʿfar aṣ-Ṣādiq ؑ:

> The believer's spirit's connection with the spirit of God is stronger than the connection of the sun's rays to the sun.[93]

There is a noticeable similarity between the Bismillāh and ṭahārah; the servant who is always in a state of ṭahārah will feel uncomfortable the instant his wuḍūʾ is voided, as if he is in a state of extreme impurity. Similarly, he who is accustomed to reciting Bismillāh before doing anything will be uneasy should he forget it before an act, and will feel deserted by his Lord Almighty. For this reason, should we forget the Bismillāh before eating and remember whilst eating, we are told to compensate for it by saying *In the Name of God* at its beginning and at its end. It is also recommended to recite the Bismillāh aloud when eating, to remind those around to do the same.

Anybody who disciplines himself to start everything, whether major or minor, with Bismillāh will eventually turn into a person who automatically and constantly evokes the Name of God ﷻ. There are so many actions and undertakings in a single day, and should a servant link every

---

[93] Kulaynī, Shaykh Muḥammad b. Yaʿqūb, *al-Kāfī*, Vol. 2, p. 166.

one of them to Bismillāh, the remembrance of God ﷻ would be infused into his everyday life, and would encompass his every movement! And that is the stage of plentiful remembrance that the greatest and most pious of believers wish to achieve.

The Name of God ﷻ contains countless secrets which the human mind cannot comprehend, as it points towards the entity that has amassed all forms of greatness and beauty. The origin of the word "God" is the word 'Ilāh', meaning 'god', which was then preceded by 'Al' to form 'Al-Ilāh', after which the letter 'I' was removed and the two 'L's put together, to form the word "God". Imām Muḥammad al-Bāqir ؑ says in a narration:

> The meaning of God is:
>
> > The One who is worshipped.
>
> Creation cannot grasp His Essence or understand His Nature.[94]

In another narration, Imām 'Alī ؑ was asked about the meaning of the word 'God', to which he responded:

[94] *at-Tawḥīd*, p. 89.

God is He in whom all take refuge in times of need and difficulty after having lost hope in all but Him, and after having broken relations with all but Him.[95]

[95] Ibid., p. 231.

# The Inner Etiquettes of Recitation

Sūrat al-Fātiḥah, also named Sūrat al-Ḥamd, is the greatest Sūrah in the Noble Qur'ān. Also known as as-Sabʿ al-Mathānī (the Seven Oft-Repeated Verses), it was deemed equivalent to the entire Qur'ān, and all prayers were made to include this Holy Sūrah. But, shockingly, the worshipper may read this Sūrah at least ten times a day without truly thinking through its values, nor those of Sūrat al-Ikhlāṣ. The truth is that we are ordered in the Qur'ān itself to contemplate its meanings, including the Sūrahs recited during prayer, when God ﷻ says:

﴿أَفَلَا يَتَدَبَّرُونَ ٱلْقُرْءَانَ أَمْ عَلَىٰ قُلُوبٍ أَقْفَالُهَآ﴾

*﴾a-fa-lā yatadabbarūna l-qur'āna am ʿalā qulūbin aqfāluhā﴿*

*﴾Do they not contemplate the Qur'ān, or are there locks on the hearts?﴿*[96]

and in narrations, such as the narration from the Holy Prophet ﷺ:

> There is no good in worship not known, nor is there any good in recitation not having pondering in it.[97]

---

[96] Sūrat Muḥammad, Verse 24.

[97] Majlisī, ʿAllāmah Muḥammad Bāqir, *Biḥār al-Anwār*, Vol. 75, p. 74.

The Bismillāh is an inseparable part of Sūrat al-Fātiḥah, and one of the signs of a believer is to recite it out loud, as narrated from Imām al-Ḥasan al-ʿAskarī 🕮. In essence, it is an internal statement of servitude, where the servant commences every action he does, even if trivial, with the Bismillāh. And saying it out loud is a declaration of this servitude, where the servant opens his communications with his Lord with the help of the Bismillāh. Without its help, the servant would have no permission and no right to speak to his Lord, who holds all forms of authority over His subjects.

When the servant reaches any mention of his Almighty Lord in his prayer, he must pay full attention with his heart, for any lover's heart will flutter at the mention of the name of his beloved, as is the case with those in love with mortals, let alone those in love with the Divine. And do not doubt that the Lord Almighty Himself reciprocates this heartfelt evocation of God's Name from the servant. However, the servant's love is nowhere near comparable to that of the Almighty Lord!

Through Sūrat al-Fātiḥah, God 🕮 wishes to teach His servant the courtesy of talking to the Lord of creation, as is evident through the fact that the Sūrah is spoken in the words of the servant. Whatever amount of effort and time the servant puts into choosing words of servitude and subordination, he will always be failed by his own limitations, which is why some recommend that one recites

﴿إِيَّاكَ نَعْبُدُ وَإِيَّاكَ نَسْتَعِينُ﴾

*﴾iyyāka naʿbudu wa-ʾiyyāka nastaʿīnu﴿*

*﴾You [alone] do we worship, and to You [alone] do we turn for help﴿*[98]

during every supplication, because these words were put together by the Almighty, and meant for the Almighty.

Out of all His Great Names, God ﷻ chose the two names associated with mercy, which the servant recites four times in Sūrat al-Fātiḥah, which shows that the principle of mercy is the foundation of all good in this world. The primary step in obtaining this abundant Divine mercy is for the servant to imitate his Lord in this trait as perfectly as humanly possible, whether it is the mercy to all creation he is emulating, or the mercy exclusive to faithful believers. Truly, the servant who gains this trait is the person capable of receiving God's ﷻ merciful gaze, a distinct result of which is God's special attention to him during prayer.

The principle of mercy is repeated sixty times every day during daily prayers, and so we must question the state of a servant that does not hold in his heart any mercy towards other servants; does he truly expect his prayers to be answered?! Indeed, what is required from the servant is

---

[98] Sūrat al-Fātiḥah, Verse 5.

grander than that; he should have the ability to forgive those who have oppressed him, just as God ﷻ says,

﴿وَلْيَعْفُوا۟ وَلْيَصْفَحُوٓا۟ ۗ أَلَا تُحِبُّونَ أَن يَغْفِرَ ٱللَّهُ لَكُمْ﴾

*﴿wa-l-yaʿfū wa-l-yaṣfaḥū a-lā tuḥibbūna an yaghfira llāhu lakum﴾*

*﴿and let them excuse and forbear. Do you not love that God should forgive you?﴾*[99]

Furthermore, the promised reward for this trait is the same as that value, meaning God's ﷻ pardon for he who pardons his brother in faith.

Ḥamd is praise for something someone did by choice, while complimenting is praise for something they may have done voluntarily or involuntarily. When we say "Alḥamdulilāh" (All praise is for God), the article 'the' here is for totality, meaning that all praise is exclusive to God ﷻ. All good accomplished by those other than Him is by his authorisation. Therefore, the servant's gratitude to his Lord Almighty must be accompanied by a sense of shame that stimulates him to work to repay his Lord and make up for his shortcomings. This stimulation is the practical outcome of ḥamd, and it is greater than any simple praise uttered by the tongue, even if complemented with thoughts of gratitude.

---

[99] Sūrat an-Nūr, Verse 22.

The first lesson we learn from expressing gratitude to God directly after Bismillāh is that one must accustom oneself to appreciate the blessings bestowed upon them. We first turn to God ﷻ to declare our gratefulness towards Him, and then we turn to His delegates, His devoted servants, who deliver these blessings to us, and thank them for their kindness. It is narrated that Imām 'Alī ar-Riḍā ؑ said:

> Whoever is ungrateful for the blessings from the created ones is not grateful to God, the Honourable, the Exalted.[100]

After alluding to His Divinity, which entails His command over all creation, God ﷻ refers to the attribute of His Ownership of the Day of Judgement, or His Power on that Day, depending on the interpretation of the Holy Verse. Either way, this attribute is cited as a direct reason for His Divinity and command, as it is caused by His being the owner or sovereign of His servants in the literal sense, rather than in the figurative sense. And should the worshipper truly contemplate the implications of this, he would really feel a sense of peace and assurance, for he would see himself connected to the One who has control over everything. He would lose that arrogance and conceit after realising all his worship is to the One who exclusively holds dominion over everyone and everything.

---

[100] Ṣadūq, Shaykh Muḥammad b. 'Alī, *'Uyūn Akhbār al-Riḍā* ؑ, Vol. 2, p. 24.

The Arabic word ʿalam (world) is used to describe the subject of ʿilm (knowledge), as opposed to the word ʿalam (knowledgeable), which is used to describe the receiver of ʿilm. Hence, the word ʿalam encompasses all creation. And so when we describe God ﷻ as "Rabb al-ʿĀlamīn" (the Lord of All the Worlds), one can only imagine the power of the One who controls all these worlds and all their variations. Is submitting to anybody but Him not shameless?! All these worlds and creations are finite, limited, leaving nothing but the Glory of their Creator, and it is He who endears Himself to His servants through this blessed Sūrah.

The different recurring expressions of praise that the servant utters during prayer have their own separate worlds and realms. On the surface, it does not cost the worshipper anything more than a simple movement of the lips as he utters two soft words, saying "Alḥamdulilāh", whether in Sūrat al-Fātiḥah or elsewhere. But these words have a realm of their own, just like the Bismillāh, and contain secrets only known by somebody whom the Noble Qur'ān has spoken to directly. As the Holy Prophet ﷺ says in a narration,

> If a servant says 'Praise be to God', it would be weightier on his scale than the seven heavens and the seven earths.[101]

[101] Ṭabrisī, Mīrzā Ḥusayn Nūrī, *Mustadrak al-Wasā'il wa-Mustanbaṭ al-Masā'il*, Vol. 5, p. 314.

And, in another narration from him ﷺ, he says:

> If the entire world were in the hands of a man of my nation, and he said, 'Praise be to God', that praise would be better than all of that.[102]

After the worshipper has acknowledged that his Lord is exclusively deserving of "gratitude" first, and that his Lord is "divine" and holds all power and command second, and that He, Almighty, holds the trait of "mercy" both inclusive and exclusive third, and that He is in "possession" of the Day of Judgement fourth, he then speaks to His Lord directly, saying "*You [alone] do we worship, and to You [alone] do we turn for help*". Indeed, does any other being than He who holds these traits and qualities deserve to be worshipped or turned to?! It is as if the entire Sūrah progresses from the introductions all the way to the results, from causes to effects.

The sudden switch from the third person to the second person form of speech in the verse

﴿إِيَّاكَ نَعْبُدُ وَإِيَّاكَ نَسْتَعِينُ﴾

﴿*iyyāka naʿbudu wa-ʾiyyāka nastaʿīnu*﴾

[102] *Nawādir al-Uṣūl*, Vol. 2, p. 267.

﴾*You [alone] do we worship, and to You [alone] do we turn for help*﴿[103]

holds a very deep meaning; that the worshipper must pass through a few prefaces before entering the sanctuary of God ﷻ, by which he earns the privilege of witnessing his Almighty Lord before him, and talking directly to his Lord like a person talks to his confidant. This is as mentioned in the qudsī narration:

> I am the companion of he who speaks of Me.[104]

After the servant has declared that he worships nobody and turns to nobody but his Almighty Lord, he is now entitled to request from his Lord to guide him to the Ṣirāṭ al-Mustaqīm (the Straight Path). Should the servant take this Path successfully in this world, he will certainly pass the Ṣirāṭ on the Day of Judgement successfully as well. However, if one is insincere in his claim of exclusive worship to God ﷻ, then he is incapable of being guided to the Straight Path, regardless of the number of times he repeats his request, because he has not followed the specific guidelines so clearly set in this Sūrah.

The secret to internal closeness to God ﷻ can be summed up in three words: fear, love, and hope. All three of these can be established through Sūrat al-Fātiḥah; fear through

---

[103] Sūrat al-Fātiḥah, Verse 5.

[104] Kulaynī, Shaykh Muḥammad b. Yaʿqūb, *al-Kāfī*, Vol. 2, p. 496.

indicating God's ﷻ supremacy on the Day of Judgement; love through pointing out that true worship is to nobody but Him, as true submission to God ﷻ stems from one's love towards Him; hope through declaring that only He is whom to turn to for help, as everything is in His hand, and everyone is empowered through Him only.

There is only one Straight Path, one Ṣirāṭ al-Mustaqīm, but there are different ways to reach it. The roads to God ﷻ are as abundant as creation itself, but the problem lies in the fact that the servant may not take the best road. This is something exclusive to the greatest and most resilient of monotheists, whom God ﷻ has guided to their own paths, as pointed out by God ﷻ Himself:

﴿وَٱلَّذِينَ جَٰهَدُواْ فِينَا لَنَهۡدِيَنَّهُمۡ سُبُلَنَاۚ وَإِنَّ ٱللَّهَ لَمَعَ ٱلۡمُحۡسِنِينَ﴾

﴾*wa-lladhīna jāhadū fīnā la-nahdiyannahum subulanā wa-'inna llāha la-ma'a l-muḥsinīna*﴿

﴾*As for those who strive in Us, We shall surely guide them in Our ways, and God is indeed with the virtuous*﴿[105]

A worshipper may choose a path towards servitude, unaware that the closer route that God ﷻ wants him to take is a completely different path that he hasn't thought of. And the best way to explain this is what God ﷻ said from the viewpoint of His Prophet Sulaymān ﷺ:

---

105 Sūrat al-'Ankabūt, Verse 69.

﴿وَأَنْ أَعْمَلَ صَٰلِحًا تَرْضَىٰهُ﴾

*﴿wa-'an a'mala ṣāliḥan tarḍāhu﴾*

*﴿and that I may do righteous deeds which please You﴾*[106]

Ss in: righteous deeds approved by God ﷻ, not just any righteous deeds.

In Sūrat al-Fātiḥah, after praising God ﷻ, submitting to Him, and seeking assistance from Him, the servant asks his Lord for guidance. Not to take him to the objective, but rather to direct him to the path towards it. The job of the Holy Prophets ﷺ was to reveal the path, but reaching the objective relies on the effort of the servant himself. This has been God's ﷻ system throughout history, and whoever thinks that this system will change for him, and that he will be transported to the objective without any effort of his own, is, in fact, dreaming and unaware of the philosophy of creation.

The Holy Sūrah ends on a scary note, which is: he who God ﷻ has not blessed is deluded, even if his ignorance is multi-layered, in that he does not know that he does not know, and even if he is not purposefully taking the incorrect path. On the other hand, he who neglects learning about the true path is among those who have

[106] Sūrat an-Naml, Verse 19.

incurred God's ﷻ wrath, which is severer than mere delusion.

The key to being guided and following the true path is to understand how much of a blessing it is to know it. However much the servant tries to find out what is hidden on this path himself, he will remain lost and eluded, as the Noble Qur'ān says:

﴿وَلَوْلَا فَضْلُ ٱللَّهِ عَلَيْكُمْ وَرَحْمَتُهُۥ لَٱتَّبَعْتُمُ ٱلشَّيْطَٰنَ إِلَّا قَلِيلًا﴾

*﴿wa-law-lā faḍlu llāhi 'alaykum wa-raḥmatuhū la-ttaba'tumu sh-shayṭāna illā qalīlan﴾*

*﴿And were it not for God's grace upon you and His mercy, you would have surely followed Shayṭān, [all] except a few﴾*[107]

Those fortunate enough to receive this blessing, however, are the privileged servants of God ﷻ, as He Almighty says:

﴿وَمَن يُطِعِ ٱللَّهَ وَٱلرَّسُولَ فَأُو۟لَٰٓئِكَ مَعَ ٱلَّذِينَ أَنْعَمَ ٱللَّهُ عَلَيْهِم مِّنَ ٱلنَّبِيِّـۧنَ وَٱلصِّدِّيقِينَ وَٱلشُّهَدَآءِ وَٱلصَّٰلِحِينَ ۚ وَحَسُنَ أُو۟لَٰٓئِكَ رَفِيقًا﴾

*﴿wa-man yuṭi'i llāha wa-r-rasūla fa-'ulā'ika ma'a lladhīna an'ama llāhu 'alayhim mina n-nabiyyīna wa-ṣ-ṣiddīqīna wa-sh-shuhadā'i wa-ṣ-ṣāliḥīna wa-ḥasuna ulā'ika rafīqan﴾*

---

[107] Sūrat an-Nisā', Verse 83.

﴾*Whoever obeys God and the Apostle—they are with those whom God has blessed, including the prophets and the truthful, the martyrs and the righteous, and excellent companions are they!*﴿[108]

It is truly striking that one may reach an age of sixty years, and recite the duʿāʾ in Sūrat al-Fātiḥah for guidance from God ﷻ every day of those sixty years, and still not see any sign of that request being granted. He does not find himself on the Straight Path, but instead sees himself in an erratic and unhinged position, feeling that internal vexation felt by those who are astray, or those who have incurred God's ﷻ wrath.

Sūrat al-Fātiḥah is comparable to a conversation between the worshipper and his Lord. Although God ﷻ Himself puts together the entire Sūrah, it is actually in two parts: The first part is the worshipper's proclamation of his Lord's traits, until the verse "*Master of the Day of Retribution*":

﴿بِسۡمِ ٱللَّهِ ٱلرَّحۡمَٰنِ ٱلرَّحِيمِ﴾

﴾*bi-smi llāhi r-raḥmāni r-raḥīm*[1]﴿

﴿ٱلۡحَمۡدُ لِلَّهِ رَبِّ ٱلۡعَٰلَمِينَ﴾

---

[108] Sūrat an-Nisāʾ, Verse 69.

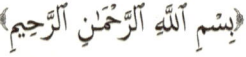

﴿*al-ḥamdu li-llāhi rabbi l-ʿālamīna*﴾

﴿ٱلرَّحۡمَٰنِ ٱلرَّحِيمِ﴾

﴿*A r-raḥmāni r-raḥīmi*﴾

﴿مَٰلِكِ يَوۡمِ ٱلدِّينِ﴾

﴿*māliki yawmi d-dīni*﴾

﴿*In the Name of God, the Beneficent, the Merciful. All praise belongs to God, Lord of all the worlds, the Beneficent, the Merciful, Master of the Day of Retribution*﴾[109]

And then, starting at "*You [alone] do we worship, and to You [alone] do we turn for help*" it switches to the worshipper talking directly to his Almighty Lord.

﴿إِيَّاكَ نَعۡبُدُ وَإِيَّاكَ نَسۡتَعِينُ﴾

﴿*iyyāka naʿbudu wa-ʾiyyāka nastaʿīnu*﴾

﴿ٱهۡدِنَا ٱلصِّرَٰطَ ٱلۡمُسۡتَقِيمَ﴾

﴿*ihdinā ṣ-ṣirāṭa l-mustaqīma*﴾

---

[109] Sūrat al-Fātiḥah, Verses 1–4.

﴿صِرَٰطَ ٱلَّذِينَ أَنْعَمْتَ عَلَيْهِمْ غَيْرِ ٱلْمَغْضُوبِ عَلَيْهِمْ وَلَا ٱلضَّآلِّينَ﴾

*﴾ṣirāṭa lladhīna anʿamta ʿalayhim ghayri l-maghḍūbi ʿalayhim wa-lā ḍ-ḍāllīna﴿*

*﴾You [alone] do we worship, and to You [alone] do we turn for help. Guide us on the straight path, the path of those whom You have blessed — such as have not incurred Your wrath, nor are astray﴿*[110]

Sūrat al-Ikhlāṣ, also known as Sūrat al-Tawḥīd, is equivalent to a third of the entire Qurʾān, according to narrations. This has been interpreted in two ways:

a) considering the reward of reciting this Sūrat, which would be equal to the reward of reciting a third of the Noble Qurʾān, or

b) considering this meaning, as we have the Uṣūl ad-Dīn, which are Tawḥīd, Nubuwwah, and Maʿād, (Imāmate can be considered a derivative of Nubuwwah, and ʿAdl can be considered a derivative of Tawḥīd, hence the reason why we counted three Uṣūl ad-Dīn instead of five), and since this Sūrah discusses Tawḥīd, it equates a third of the Qurʾān.

In fact, what prevents both these meanings from being true?

---

110 Sūrat al-Fātiḥah, Verses 5–7.

Despite being very brief, Sūrat al-Ikhlāṣ contains deep secrets that the average person cannot comprehend, because it includes the definition of God's ﷻ Divinity, which is not an easy theme to understand. The pronoun 'He' at the beginning of the Sūrah indicates His being in the realm of the unknown, whereas the Name 'God' is a collective Name encompassing all His traits.

Sūrat al-Ikhlāṣ is considered one of the four qalaaqil (so called because they all start with the word "Qul", meaning 'say'), which are Sūrat al-Kāfirūn, Sūrat al-Ikhlāṣ, Sūrat al-Falaq, and Sūrat an-Nās. It has been said that these four Sūrahs talk to the Holy Prophet more directly than other verses and Sūrah, because, although the verb "Qul" is implied in every verse in the Noble Qur'ān, these Sūrahs explicitly use the verb to emphasise the necessity of contemplating the connotations of these Sūrahs.

What is being established in the first verse,

﴿قُلْ هُوَ ٱللَّهُ أَحَدٌ﴾

﴿*qul huwa llāhu aḥad^un-i^*﴾

﴿*Say, 'He is God, the One'*﴾[111]

[111] Sūrat al-Ikhlāṣ, Verse 1.

is His singularity, not His oneness, because denying that something is one does not necessarily deny its possible plurality. In other words, when somebody says 'There is not a single person in the house', they mean that no human exists in the house, whereas, if somebody says 'There is not one person in the house', there is a possibility that there are two or more people in the house.

One of the best places to repeatedly recite this blessed Sūrah is during ṭawāf, because ṭawāf is a monotheistic act; the servant recites this Sūrah from the moment he makes Iḥrām in ash-Shajarah Mosque until he finishes the rituals of Ḥajj or 'Umrah. As for timing, the best time to recite this Sūrah is during the holy month of Ramaḍān, for every verse recited in this month is equivalent to an entire khatmah, and reciting this Sūrah three times is also equivalent to a khatmah, so that one can imagine the vast rewards caused by this brief recitation!

Stating that God ﷻ is the sustainer of creation in the Holy verse:

﴿ٱللَّهُ ٱلصَّمَدُ﴾

﴿*allāhu ṣ-ṣamadu*﴾

﴿*God is the Embracing*﴾[112]

---

[112] Sūrat al-Ikhlāṣ, Verse 2.

and denying that He is part of a whole in the next verse

﴿لَمْ يَلِدْ وَلَمْ يُولَدْ﴾

*﴿lam yalid wa-lam yūlad﴾*

*﴿He neither begat, nor was begotten﴾*[113]

are two sides of a single truth. Describing God ﷻ as a constituent of a whole would imply that He needs the other components to complete Him. In contrast, the Eternal Absolute is the refuge and supplier of all needs, and does not require anything else at all. There is another meaning of the word 'Ṣamad': a solid with no cavities, i.e., not hollow. And what we learn from this meaning is that God ﷻ is not separated into an exterior and an interior, for that is the characteristic of hollow things, and God ﷻ is exalted above such descriptions.

During the third and fourth rakʿahs in prayer, the worshipper can choose to either recite Sūrat al-Fātiḥah or recite the four tasbīḥāt, "Subḥān Allāh, Wa-l-ḥamdu li-llāh, Wa lā ilāha illā Allāh, Wa-llāhu Akbar" (Glory belongs to God, all praise belongs to God, there is no god but God, and God is greater), which goes to show the greatness of these tasbīḥāt, which, as is narrated from Imām Jaʿfar aṣ-Ṣādiq ؑ, form the foundations of al-ʿArsh.

---

113 Sūrat al-Ikhlāṣ, Verse 3.

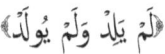

It is possible to combine the recurring praise for God ﷻ, and the denial of lowly traits from Him, in the four tasbīḥāt and during rukūʿ and sujūd, with the sense of frailty felt during munājāt and conversation with God ﷻ. This is possible through picturing the different ways the lowly human has transgressed on his Almighty Lord, to the point where he has associated with God ﷻ what would cause the universe to quake and the mountains to collapse, as God ﷻ says:

﴿تَكَادُ ٱلسَّمَٰوَٰتُ يَتَفَطَّرۡنَ مِنۡهُ وَتَنشَقُّ ٱلۡأَرۡضُ وَتَخِرُّ ٱلۡجِبَالُ هَدًّا﴾

﴿*takādu s-samāwātu yatafaṭṭarna minhu wa-tanshaqqu l-ʾarḍu wa-takhirru l-jibālu hadda*$^{n}$﴾

﴿أَن دَعَوۡاْ لِلرَّحۡمَٰنِ وَلَدٗا﴾

﴿*an daʿaw li-r-raḥmāni walada*﴾

﴿*The heavens are about to be rent apart at it, the earth to split open, and the mountains to collapse into bits, that they should ascribe a son to the Beneficent!*﴾[114]

The true lover of God ﷻ feels pain and sorrow when witnessing such disrespect from others towards his magnificent beloved. And one can imagine the way God ﷻ looks at His servant, who is in such a state of spirituality

---

[114] Sūrat Maryam, Verses 90–91.

when refuting such attributes from God, as if he is embarrassed that this rudeness would come from his fellow humans.

Another fitting sensation one should feel while praising his Almighty Lord in prayer is a sense of shame within himself, for the prayer he offers is unworthy of Him whom he stands before. It is like he is saying, "Lord Almighty!" You are dignified above my lowly and empty worship that is riddled with shortcomings and inattention, caused by none other than my own shortcomings. This reflects what is said during the Yūnusī Tasbīḥ, "Lā ilāha illā Anta subḥānaka innī kuntu minaẓ-ẓālimīn" (There is no god except You! You are immaculate! I have indeed been among the wrongdoers!), and also what is said during taʿqīb, where the worshipper says:

> My Lord, if there is a defect or a deficiency in my prayer, whether in bowing or prostration, then do not reproach me...[115]

After reciting tasbīḥ, ḥamd, and tahlīl in the four tasbīḥāt, the worshipper concludes it all with takbīr, as if he is stating that, even after all this praise and acclaim, he remains unable to truly describe God ﷻ as is worthy of His Glory. So he says, "God is Greater," to express this inability to describe Him Almighty, which is truly the utmost description.

---

[115] Qummī, Shaykh ʿAbbās, *Mafātīḥ al-Jinān*.

And here, it is necessary to emphasise that it is most suitable for the worshipper to repeat the four tasbīḥāt three times in each of the last two rakʿahs, even though reciting it only once is technically admissible. But by doing so, the worshipper misses out on vast amounts of irreplaceable rewards, for it is narrated that Imām Jaʿfar aṣ-Ṣādiq ﷺ said while advising his wives and family:

> Do not say in your rukūʿ and sujūd less than three tasbīḥ, for if you do so, it would not be the best act from you.[116]

One of the traps Shayṭān sets for worshippers, specifically those working on perfecting the external aspect of prayer, is to have the worshipper concentrate so much on the articulation of the letters, known as Makhārij al-Ḥurūf, that it becomes an obsession. He gets carried away by the realm of words and pronunciation, and completely overlooks the realm of meanings. Whilst the latter brings earnestness and sincerity to prayer, the former leads to neglecting prayer's essence and ultimately to turning away from prayer altogether.

---

[116] Majlisī, ʿAllāmah Muḥammad Bāqir, *Biḥār al-Anwār*, Vol. 82, p. 120.

# The Inner Etiquettes of Rukūʿ

After reciting Sūrat al-Fātiḥah and another Sūrah, the worshipper then bows in front of his Almighty Lord in rukūʿ. Before and after rukūʿ, the worshipper says "Allāhu Akbar", as though this takbīr is an alarm bell bringing the worshipper back to his senses, and reminding him that God ﷻ is greater than to be described! And, as such, the appearance of the worshipper must correspond with this great slogan dispersed throughout the prayer.

Something very interesting we find in prayer is the focus on a particular supplication, which is the ṣalawāt, "Allāhumma ṣalli ʿalā Muḥammad wa Āli Muḥammad" (Oh God, send your blessings upon Muḥammad, and the Family of Muḥammad). During the entirety of prayer, there is only one wājib request that must be made, which is the request for guidance in Sūrat al-Fātiḥah. There is also only one mustaḥabb request, which is the ṣalawāt, which the worshipper repeats during his rukūʿ, sujūd, qunūt (where he recites ṣalawāt before and after his own supplication), and during tashahhud.

For so long, we have prayed and bowed in such blessed locations: behind the ḥaṭīm, behind the maqām, under the mīzāb, and at the ḥā'ir, but this rukūʿ of ours has not been in its true form. For he who lives within the glorious light of his Lord will find his rukūʿ connected to this infinite light, and all the glory and magnificence it contains. By being a step before sujūd, rukūʿ becomes almost a prelude to entering the realm of closeness with God ﷻ, like meeting the emperors of this world. And so rukūʿ has the aroma of respect and veneration, while sujūd holds the scent of proximity to God ﷻ. And should the worshipper succeed and excel in his respect and veneration, he would be closer to the exclusive circle of divine proximity.

Behind the physical bowing involved in rukūʿ is a certain spiritual principle, where the worshipper feels that sense of humility before his Almighty Lord. Similarly, when a prison guard wants to humiliate a prisoner, he takes his head. He lowers it down until the prisoner reaches a bowing state, and should he want to degrade him further, forces him to lower his head all the way to the ground in a state of prostration. It is very sad, however, to see somebody's rukūʿ of worship and spirituality eventually transform into a mere physical bow, void of any spiritual value!

The true foundation of rukoo is the tasbīḥ, which is exactly what Prophet Yūnus ﷺ included in his supplication in the whale's belly. And tasbīḥ has two perspectives: sometimes it is about exalting God ﷻ above all flaws and imperfections, and all the claims made by deniers throughout history, and sometimes the worshipper means to exalt his Lord Almighty about his own actions. When the worshipper finds himself in a dilemma, the first thing he does is state that his Lord Almighty is above oppression and injustice, and instead puts the blame on himself for his own shortcomings.

After completing his rukūʿ, the worshipper then returns to a standing position as a wājib step in prayer, which shows the importance of this checkpoint in prayer despite having no obligatory dhikr. Thus, one should contemplate the mustaḥabb dhikr here, as we are told to say "Samiʿa Allāhu liman ḥamidah" (God has heard to him who praised Him). The dhikr here is in the past tense, meaning that the praise has, in fact, happened. The addition of 'to' is to communicate that this praise has been answered. And people who have been answered to include anybody on Earth who praises Him. In this sense, every servant who prays actually offers prayer to other worshippers, in a way that all other worshippers pray for him too. Imagine how everybody prays for one another, as long as they are praising God ﷻ, in every prayer, all at the same time.

During rukūʿ and sujūd, the worshipper's vision becomes limited, such that he sees nothing in front of him, as opposed to when he is in a standing position in Qiyām. Hence, this involuntary visual barrier to distractions can help him regain some focus in his prayer as he looks between his feet during rukūʿ, and at the tip of his nose in sujūd. Additionally, this lowering of the head, done exclusively for God ﷻ, adds to the feeling of humility and submissiveness towards the Almighty Lord, should the servant truly understand its value, undeterred by the habits that prevent him from recognizing its meaning.

Symbolism is present in prayer from the beginning to the end, just like all other acts of worship. And it is the Ahl al-Bayt ﷺ who truly understood what each action represents, for just as the Qur'ān is only comprehended by those addressed by it, the reality of prayer is only truly grasped by those who communicate with God ﷻ with true knowledge. In this context, Imām ʿAlī ؑ was asked about the meaning of extending the neck in rukūʿ, to which he replied:

> Its interpretation is,
>
> > I believe in Your Oneness, even if my neck were to be severed.[117]

When we recite the dhikr during rukūʿ, "Subḥāna Rabbī al-ʿAẓīm wa bi-ḥamdih" (Glory is to my Lord, the Great, and all praise belongs to Him), the 'Bi' added to 'Ḥamd' in "Bi-ḥamdih" has several possible meanings:

Accompaniment: as in: I glorify my Lord while praising Him.

Usage: as in: I glorify my Lord by praising Him.

Adornment: as in: I exalt my Lord above all imperfection as I praise Him.

In several instances in the Noble Qur'ān, we are ordered to glorify God ﷻ, and as such, reciting tasbīḥ in our rukūʿ and sujūd is deemed as compliance to this Divine command in the Holy Book, in addition to it being a wājib dhikr in prayer. It is narrated that when the verse

---

[117] Majlisī, ʿAllāmah Muḥammad Bāqir, *Biḥār al-Anwār*, Vol. 81, p. 361.

﴿فَسَبِّحۡ بِٱسۡمِ رَبِّكَ ٱلۡعَظِيمِ﴾

*﴿fa-sabbiḥ bi-smi rabbika l-ʿaẓīmi﴾*

*﴿So celebrate the Name of your Lord, the Supreme﴾*[118]

was revealed, the Holy Prophet ﷺ said:

> Make it to be in your bowing.

And when

﴿سَبِّحِ ٱسۡمَ رَبِّكَ ٱلۡأَعۡلَى﴾

*﴿sabbiḥi sma rabbika l-ʾaʿlā﴾*

*﴿Celebrate the Name of your Lord, the Most Exalted﴾*[119]

was revealed, the Holy Prophet ﷺ said:

> Make it to be in your prostration.[120]

---

[118] Sūrat al-Wāqiʿah, Verse 74.

[119] Sūrat al-Aʿlā, Verse 1.

[120] Ṣadūq, Shaykh Muḥammad b. ʿAlī, *ʿIlal al-Sharāiʿ*, Vol. 2, p. 333.

# The Inner Etiquettes of Sujūd[121]

Sujūd is one of the most important parts of prayer, for in it the worshipper is the closest he can be to his Almighty Lord. It is as if all the steps, from the takbīr to the recitation of Sūrat al-Fātiḥah and the second Sūrah, to the rukūʿ and the Qiyām, all lead up to this moment of proximity to God ﷻ, just as Imām Jaʿfar aṣ-Ṣādiq ؑ said:

> There is courtesy in bowing, and in prostration nearness to God.[122]

For making a mistake in the previous stages is a form of disrespect that prevents the proximity yearned for in sujūd.

There are different types of prostration, including:

The ethereal prostration of all beings: meaning their submission to God ﷻ as part of their natural existence, for God ﷻ gave everything its creation, and then guided it, and He has said:

﴿وَلِلَّهِ يَسۡجُدُ مَن فِي ٱلسَّمَٰوَٰتِ وَٱلۡأَرۡضِ طَوۡعٗا وَكَرۡهٗا وَظِلَٰلُهُم بِٱلۡغُدُوِّ وَٱلۡأٓصَالِ۩﴾

121 ۩ This upcoming symbol in the Noble Qur'ān indicates an āyah of sajdah (verse of prostration). When recited or heard, performing sujūd (prostration) is mandatory (wājib) for specific verses and recommended (mustaḥabb) for others.

122 Imām Jaʿfar aṣ-Ṣādiq ؑ, *Miṣbāḥ al-Sharīʿah*, p. 89.

*﴾wa-li-llāhi yasjudu man fī s-samāwāti wa-l-ʾarḍi ṭawʿan wa-karhan wa-ẓilāluhum bi-l-ghuduwwi wa-l-ʾāṣāl﴿*

*﴾To God prostrates whoever there is in the heavens and the earth, willingly or unwillingly, and their shadows at sunrise and sunset﴿*[123]

The physical prostration of the servant during prayer, which involves placing the seven body parts—being the forehead, palms, knees, and toes—on the ground.

The internal prostration: a spiritual state marked by awe, humility, love, and an intent gaze at the glorious and perfect aspect of God ﷻ. And, undoubtedly, whoever reaches this stage of enjoyment of God's ﷻ presence considers sujūd an opportunity of an indescribable journey towards the realm of the unseen.

There are some instances in the servant's material or otherworldly life in which he needs things that could change the trajectory of his entire existence if they were given to him. Therefore, he should use sujūd to present his needs before the Almighty. And one of the renowned methods to attain satisfaction of such needs is what is narrated from Imām Jaʿfar aṣ-Ṣādiq ؑ:

> If a worshiper stands before his Lord in the middle of the night, prays four units deep into a night, prostrates

123 Sūrat ar-Raʿd, Verse 15.

a prostration of gratitude (Sujūd ash-Shukr) after completing his prayer, then says:

> Whatever God wills, whatever God wills (Mā shā'a Llāh, Mā shā'a Llāh)

One hundred times, God calls to him from above him:

> O My servant! How long will you say
>
> Whatever God wills, whatever God wills?!
>
> I am your Lord, and the definite Will is Mine. I have decided to fulfil your need, so ask me for whatever you wish.[124]

Something that leads to gratification during sujūd is to accustom oneself to prostrating to God ﷻ whenever a blessing is remembered or granted. And it should not be forgotten that God's blessings on His servants are countless, and each requires its own sujūd. And so it turns into an unbreakable bond, as a relationship is created between blessings and sujūd, and what a beautiful relationship that is!

Sometimes, one may fall asleep during his sujūd, leading him to feel it was an hour wasted in his life, when in reality, he was in the hospitality of God ﷻ. It is even possible that, in that state, he was given blessings that outnumber

[124] Ṣadūq, Shaykh Muḥammad b. 'Alī, *al-Amālī*, p. 239.

anything he receives while awake, for the soul ascends to God ﷻ both in sleep and in death. And what prevents God ﷻ from returning the souls of some of His servants, after they receive His Divine outpourings in that meeting that they didn't even sense in their sleep?

During sujūd, the servant should be creative in his act of prostration. There is nothing wrong with rubbing his forehead, cheeks, and brow in the dirt to emphasise his humility as he places his most dignified part, being his head, on the most insignificant thing in this world, being dirt. Indeed, the Holy Prophets عليهم السلام had such a profound presence in sujūd, known only to God ﷻ.

Focusing one's gaze on the place of sujūd can be an incentive and a reminder for the servant to reminisce about his previous instances of sincerity that he is now missing. Additionally, repeatedly prostrating on the same specific place imbues that place with special holiness, let alone if that point of sujūd was the turbah of Imām al-Ḥusayn عليه السلام! The same turbah that never left Imām Jaʿfar aṣ-Ṣādiq عليه السلام's prayer area, as he would never prostrate on anything other than the turbah of Imām al-Ḥusayn عليه السلام, out of humility and submission to God ﷻ.

God ﷻ chose prostration when He tested the angels' obedience after creating Ādam عليه السلام, indicating that this act is the pinnacle of humility before Him. And that is what made Iblis refuse obedience on that day, for perhaps, if he was ordered to bow, for example, he may have obeyed. That is also why, when the servant wants to express his sorrows and troubles to God ﷻ, he also chooses that specific position to do so, for he is closest to his Lord in that state.

Some narrations encourage lengthening one's sujūd, a level above actually performing it, for it involves complete spiritual indulgence in the world of the soul, which provides a deeper satisfaction in the world of the unseen, pulling him away from this material realm. From here, we understand why the devotees of sujūd no longer find pleasure in the popular luxuries of this world. The narration of the Holy Prophet ﷺ is a witness to the fact that one of the effects of a prolonged sujūd is that the servant reaches the status of accompanying the Holy Prophet ﷺ himself on the Day of Judgement. What a glorious reward that is!

One of the forms of sujūd that has been proven to alleviate worry and anxiety is the Yūnusī sujūd, but if one wants to see the effects of the Yūnusī Dhikr, he must perform it in the same state as Prophet Yūnus ؑ himself. This means total submission to God ﷻ, just as Prophet Yūnus ؑ was in total submission in that darkness, the extent of which is known only by God ﷻ, deep down in the ocean, in the belly of the whale, in the middle of the night...

One of the important stations during prayer, which is lost on so many worshippers, is the istighfār we recite between the two sujūd, unaware of its deeper meanings. Istighfār is built upon a sense of regret and shame before God ﷻ. And who among us recites istighfār in such a state?! The reason for this is that we are used to reciting istighfār as a habit between sujūd, not because we are truly repentant, and it has therefore lost its meaning and spirit.

It is possible to transform the recurrent ṣalawāt we recite during rukūʿ, sujūd, and tashahhud into true supplications, instead of mere iterations we repeat, unconscious to any deeper meanings whatsoever. What is required is for the servant to request blessings upon the Holy Prophet and His Household ﷺ as if he were requesting them for himself.

The true lover of worship does not await an obligatory sujūd, such as during the prayer, or Sujūd at-Tilāwah, Sujūd as-Sahw, or Sujūd ash-Shukr to get closer to his Lord. Instead, he prostrates to his Lord out of humility or glorification, or rather because it is proper and an act of worship; rather, it is one of the greatest and most profound acts of worship. In fact, there is nothing more harrowing for Iblis than to see a descendant of Ādam ﵇ prostrating, for Iblis was ordered to prostrate, and he refused, whereas this person obeyed and was spared.

There are fifteen instances in the Noble Qur'ān in which sujūd is either wājib or mustaḥabb. It is as if the servant feels the need to emulate the prostrators whenever they are mentioned in the Noble Qur'ān. Sometimes, sujūd is associated with the sincere worshippers, such as in the Holy Verse:

﴿إِذَا تُتْلَىٰ عَلَيْهِمْ ءَايَٰتُ ٱلرَّحْمَٰنِ خَرُّوا۟ سُجَّدًا وَبُكِيًّا۩﴾

*﴿idhā tutlā ʿalayhim āyātu r-raḥmāni kharrū sujjadan wa-bukiyyaⁿ﴾*

*﴿When the signs of the Beneficent were recited to them, they would fall down weeping in prostration﴾*[125]

and sometimes to the devoted angels, as in the Holy Verse:

﴿إِنَّ ٱلَّذِينَ عِندَ رَبِّكَ لَا يَسْتَكْبِرُونَ عَنْ عِبَادَتِهِۦ وَيُسَبِّحُونَهُۥ وَلَهُۥ يَسْجُدُونَ۩﴾

*﴿inna lladhīna ʿinda rabbika lā yastakbirūna ʿan ʿibādatihī wa-yusabbiḥūnahū wa-lahū yasjudūnᵃ﴾*

*﴿Indeed those who are [stationed] near your Lord do not disdain to worship Him. They glorify Him and prostrate to Him﴾*[126]

and sometimes to all beings, such as in the Holy Verse:

﴿وَلِلَّهِ يَسْجُدُ مَن فِي ٱلسَّمَٰوَٰتِ وَٱلْأَرْضِ طَوْعًا وَكَرْهًا وَظِلَٰلُهُم بِٱلْغُدُوِّ وَٱلْآصَالِ۩﴾

---

[125] Sūrat Maryam, Verse 58.

[126] Sūrat al-Aʿrāf, Verse 206.

﴿*wa-li-llāhi yasjudu man fī s-samāwāti wa-l-'arḍi ṭaw'an wa-karhan wa-ẓilāluhum bi-l-ghuduwwi wa-l-'āṣāl*﴾

﴿*To God prostrates whoever there is in the heavens and the earth, willingly or unwillingly, and their shadows at sunrise and sunset*﴾[127]

We see sujūd as a simple physical obligation, performed merely by placing the seven body parts onto the ground. However, it is enveloped by so many adornments that add to its beauty and splendour, as mentioned in some Fiqh books, including the increased physical contact of the forehead and the rest of the seven body parts with the ground. It is peculiar to see how the lovers of Dunyā exhaust themselves in attempts to decorate their world with useless embellishments, but do not even think to beautify their meetings with God ﷻ with these meaningful embellishments!

Lengthening one's sujūd has been narrated to be mustaḥabb, as has filling it with plenty of tasbīḥ and dhikr. The servant who abides by this Istihbab is like a person who enters a garden filled with all forms of beauty and magnificence, as his heart prevents him from leaving such beauty in a hurry. Particularly if he is overcome by a state of tenderness accompanied by some tears, then he will be living in an indescribable world of grandeur and magnificence.

---

[127] Sūrat ar-Ra'd, Verse 15.

One of the stages in prayer that not many people can perfect is the kneeling position, known as Jilsat al-Istirāḥah, performed after the two sujūd in the first and third rakʿahs. The worshipper should be courteous in all of his actions, conforming to the exact method mandated by the Holy Legislation, even in the most precise of movements. And so, when standing up from Jilsat al-Istirāḥah, he raises his knees first, and when he lowers himself down for sujūd, he places his hands first.

When the servant is blessed with a sincere prayer, it is recommended to prostrate in Sajdat ash-Shukr, for he knows that what he has experienced is a blessing sent by God ﷻ. And gratitude undoubtedly prompts proliferation, so the servant may experience an even more intense sense of earnestness in his next prayer if he perfects this sujūd.

# The Inner Etiquettes of Tashahhud

The word tashahhud is derived from the word Shahādah, meaning 'testimony', given by a witness. A witness is a person who attests to a certain matter or event. And there are three types of testimonies: either the witness testifies to his own benefit, or he admits to something that works to his detriment, or he attests to something for the sake of truth. The tashahhud, which includes testimony to the oneness of God ﷻ and the prophethood of the Holy Prophet ﷺ, can be considered the second type of testimony. This is because attesting to such divinity necessitates the person's servitude in worship and judgments and so on, which contradicts the judgment and desire of the soul. Additionally, acknowledging the prophethood of the Holy Prophet ﷺ requires full compliance with every detail of his Holy message.

When mentioning the Holy Prophet ﷺ in tashahhud, the worshipper first describes him as a servant, then as a messenger, conveying the sense that his status as a servant qualified him to be a prophet. Without that inner state of compliance with what God ﷻ wants from him at all times, he would not have been eligible to be sent with the Divine message. After all, it is he who spent two-thirds of his life as a faithful servant of God ﷻ, to ultimately spend the last third as a prophet and a messenger!

Imām Jaʿfar aṣ-Ṣādiq ؑ invites us to recite ṣalawāt for his Holy grandfather ﷺ with full understanding of its connotations, saying:

Therefore connect prayer to Him Almighty with ṣalawāt to him ﷺ, and obedience to Him Almighty with obedience to him ﷺ, and His testimony with his ﷺ testimony.[128]

So the Imām tells us to connect our ṣalawāt on the Holy Prophet ﷺ to God's ﷻ ṣalawāt upon him. He may mean we should synchronise the two ṣalawāt, for God ﷻ and His angels confer their blessings upon the Holy Prophet ﷺ, and, in the same context, tells us to ask for His blessings upon the Holy Prophet ﷺ. Does that not mean that we should refine our prayer to a level of perfection, focus, and dedication for it to be fit to be alongside the ṣalawāt of God ﷻ and the blessed angels upon the Holy Prophet ﷺ?!

Reciting ṣalawāt upon the Holy Prophet ﷺ is wājib during tashahhud, even though some Muslims neglect it outside of prayer. Ibn Ḥajar says in his book aṣ-Ṣawāʿiq:

> Al-Dāraquṭnī and al-Bayhaqī have both released a narration:
>
> > One who performs a prayer, but does not request blessings on Muḥammad ﷺ and his Family, will not have their prayer accepted.
>
> It seems this narration is the basis of ash-Shāfiʿī's statement:

---

[128] Majlisī, ʿAllāmah Muḥammad Bāqir, Biḥār al-Anwār, Vol. 82, p. 284.

> Requesting blessings on the Household ﷷ is obligatory in prayer, just like requesting blessings on the Holy Prophet ﷺ.[129]

He also says in a different place:

And so the command is apparent in the narration.

> Say:
>
> > Allāhumma ṣalli ʿalā Muḥammad wa Āli Muḥammad (Oh God, send your blessings upon Muḥammad, and the Family of Muḥammad).

The command is apparent in obligation, according to the correct interpretation.[130]

Al-Rāzī also mentions the same truth in his tafsīr, where he says:

> Praying for the Household is a lofty position, and for that reason it has been made to conclude the tashahhud in prayer, where one says:
>
> > O God, send Your blessings on Muḥammad ﷺ and his Family ﷷ, and have mercy on Muḥammad ﷺ

---

[129] al-Haythamī, Ibn Ḥajar, *al-Ṣawāʿiq al-Muḥriqah*, p. 234.

[130] Ibid.

> and his Family ﷺ, and this glorification has not been issued for anybody other than the Household ﷺ, all of which goes to show that the love of the Family of the Holy Prophet is obligatory.[131]

It is mustaḥabb to begin the tashahhud with ḥamd, making the middle and end of the prayer two stations for thanking God ﷻ for the opportunity to pray before His Magnificence. The servant also reminds himself that God ﷻ has blessed him to be able to rise for another rakʿah by allowing his limbs to hoist him up after being in a kneeling position. And there is no doubt that this periodic expression of gratitude is a factor in the reception and answering of the prayer, for in every rakʿah, before lowering himself for sujūd, he says "Samiʿa Allāhu liman ḥamidah" (God has heard to him who praised Him). In contrast, he himself has just praised God ﷻ in his tashahhud.

Parallel to the servant's praise for his Almighty Lord in prayer is an abundance of God's ﷻ praise for His servant. And there is simply no comparison between the two types of praise, due to the vast distinction between the Everlasting and the mortal. This all owes to God's ﷻ trait of appreciation and His promise to remember His servant if the servant remembers Him. Imām al-Ḥasan al-ʿAskarī ﷺ points out this fact, as narrated from him:

---

[131] ar-Rāzī, Fakhr ad-Dīn, *Mafāṭīḥ al-Ghayb (al-Tafsīr al-Kabīr)*, Vol. 27, p. 595.

When the worshipper sits for the first tashahhud and the second tashahhud, God ﷻ says:

> O My angels! He has fulfilled My service and My worship, and he sits praising Me and sending ṣalawāt upon Muḥammad, My prophet. I shall praise him in the kingdoms of the skies and the Earth, and I shall send ṣalawāt upon his soul among the souls![132]

One of the imaginative emotions that can give the worshipper the sincerity needed in tashahhud is for him to imagine himself on the Day of Judgement, standing before his Supreme Lord, first testifying to His divinity and renouncing all forms of shirk and polytheism, then turning to the Holy Prophet ﷺ and attesting to his servitude and prophethood, then remembering the Holy Prophet's ﷺ intercession and asking God ﷻ to accept his intercession for those great sins between his people, then finally asking God ﷻ to elevate the status of His Holy Prophet ﷺ. Hence, he who lives in that deeper state in his imagination will find his heart transported to the Day of Judgement when he prays, pulling him away from his surroundings in the material world.

---

[132] Majlisī, ʿAllāmah Muḥammad Bāqir, *Biḥār al-Anwār*, Vol. 82, p. 286.

# The Inner Etiquettes of Taslīm

Anyone sending salutations to another person must pay full attention to the person being saluted; otherwise, they would be considered negligent and disrespectful. And so, if the worshipper's mind is distracted when sending salām to the Holy Prophet ﷺ at the end of the prayer, is that not considered a form of disrespect? He should at least be reprimanded for it.

The section in taslīm containing the salutations upon the Holy Prophet ﷺ is a very eloquent expression, for it consists of greetings, mercy, and blessings, each of which possesses very distinct meanings from the others. Hence, three different types of endowments are issued by God ﷻ to His Holy Prophet ﷺ in response to the worshipper's request. Have we ever contemplated these implications once in our entire lives?! And you can imagine the amount of blessings from the Divine, and the care from the Holy Messenger ﷺ one receives for performing a perfect, encompassing, and exclusive taslīm, with all its manners and conditions...?

The word 'pious servants' in the middle salām can be applied to all pious people since the time of Ādam ؑ, the vast number of whom is only known by God ﷻ. And so if blessings are issued from God ﷻ to this huge amount of people at the request of the single worshipper, what would the worshipper's reward be as a result of these salutations? Furthermore, it is known that every salām is to be answered, and every greeting has a reply, and the pious are expected to comply with this rule more than others. But all of this has a condition, which is the arrival of the salām in the first place, as it is obvious that not every greeting reaches its addressee.

The final salām is addressed in general as implied by the use of 'you', but what is certain is that it applies to those close to the servant. But how can one be sincere in this salām if those close to him have suffered because of him before the prayer, especially when he is before God ﷻ, the Lord of all creation, and the most severe of punishers? Imām Jaʿfar aṣ-Ṣādiq ؑ issues this reproval by saying:

> If those who are close to someone are not safe from him, then those furthest from him are safest. Anyone who does not establish salām on the occasions when it should be established, he means no peace and no submission: he is a liar in his salām, even if he uses it as a form of greeting among people.[133]

Taslīm represents the final moments of the prayer; therefore, the servant who truly enjoys his prayer will feel the pain of separation during these moments. The more sincere he was during prayer, the more he felt the bitterness of being detached from that aura of delight and satisfaction which he was in. And so the worshipper takes the chance between the sections of taslīm to gain even more time. Even if he is going to recite taʿqībāt, mainly Tasbīḥat az-Zahrā', after the prayer, he tries to spread that sincerity he felt

---

[133] Imām Jaʿfar aṣ-Ṣādiq ؑ, *Miṣbāḥ al-Sharīʿah*, p. 96.

during prayer all the way until he recites these blessed tasbīḥāt.

There has been a debate over the meanings of "Upon us" and "Upon you" in the final salām. Some believe that the worshipper is greeting all those around him, including the roaming angels, the members of his community, and all the worshippers praying with him if he is praying jamāʿah. In other words, he is greeting all those who are contemporary with him. So what prevents us from extending our salām to the person who holds all our livelihoods in his hand, he whose existence stabilises the Earth and the heavens, the Awaited Imām عجل الله تعالى فرجه الشريف, to whom we turn in hope that our prayers ascend alongside his, as we recite in Duʿāʾ al-Nudbah:

> And make our prayers accepted through it?

The salāmāt uttered by the worshipper in prayer are an attempt to emulate the manners of God ﷻ, the Holy Prophet ﷺ, the angels, and the faithful believers. To make them as similar as possible, we must comprehend how their salāmāt are:

The divine salām of God ﷻ: God ﷻ sends His salutations to His prophets multiple times in the Noble Qurʾān, like the Holy Verse:

﴿سَلَٰمٌ عَلَىٰ نُوحٍ فِي ٱلۡعَٰلَمِينَ﴾

﴿*salāmun ʿalā nūḥin fī l-ʿālamīn*[a]﴾

﴿*'Peace to Noah, throughout the nations!'*﴾[134]

He also issues salām in an all-inclusive form on occasions such as the Holy Verse:

﴿سَلَٰمٌ قَوۡلٗا مِّن رَّبّٖ رَّحِيمٖ﴾

﴿*salāmun qawlan min rabbin raḥīm*[in]﴾

﴿*'Peace!'—a watchword from the all-merciful Lord*﴾[135]

The salām of the devoted angels to those entering Heaven in the Holy Verse:

﴿سَلَٰمٌ عَلَيۡكُمُ ٱدۡخُلُواْ ٱلۡجَنَّةَ﴾

﴿*salāmun ʿalaykumu dkhulū l-jannata*﴾

﴿*Peace be to you! Enter paradise*﴾[136]

The salām of the Holy Prophet ﷺ upon the faithful believers in the Holy Verse:

---

[134] Sūrat aṣ-Ṣāffāt, Verse 79.

[135] Sūrat Yā Sīn, Verse 58.

[136] Sūrat an-Naḥl, Verse 32.

﴿وَإِذَا جَآءَكَ ٱلَّذِينَ يُؤْمِنُونَ بِـَٔايَـٰتِنَا فَقُلْ سَلَـٰمٌ عَلَيْكُمْ﴾

﴿*wa-'idhā jā'aka lladhīna yu'minūna bi-'āyātinā fa-qul salāmun 'alaykum*﴾

﴿*When those who have faith in Our signs come to you, say, 'Peace to you!'*﴾[137]

The salām of the faithful addressed to themselves in the Holy Verse:

﴿فَإِذَا دَخَلْتُم بُيُوتًا فَسَلِّمُوا۟ عَلَىٰٓ أَنفُسِكُمْ تَحِيَّةً مِّنْ عِندِ ٱللَّهِ﴾

﴿*fa-'idhā dakhaltum buyūtan fa-sallimū 'alā anfusikum taḥiyyatan min 'indi llāhi*﴾

﴿*So when you enter houses, greet yourselves with a salutation from God*﴾[138]

---

137 Sūrat al-An'ām, Verse 54.

138 Sūrat an-Nūr, Verse 61.

# The Inner Etiquettes of Qunūt and Taʿqīb

Although qunūt is a mustaḥabb part of prayer, the worshipper can, within it, reach a level of connection with God ﷻ that he does not achieve during the rest of his prayer. For this is the point of unrestricted and enjoyable conversation with the Lord of creation, as one can converse in any language they wish, not just in Arabic, meaning that after reciting the specific supplications and duʿāʾ for qunūt, one can speak to God ﷻ in their mother tongue. This has been proven by some in the general statement of Imām Muḥammad al-Bāqir ؑ:

> There is nothing wrong for a man to say, in his prayer, everything he can converse with his Lord Almighty with.[139]

The true believer loves to extend his qunūt to remain in conversation with his Lord for as long as possible, so what is wrong with reciting Duʿāʾ Kumayl in his qunūt on Friday nights?! Or busying himself with the recitation of Duʿāʾ Abū Ḥamza Thumālī in his Night Prayers, or even in his wājib prayers?! It is narrated that the Holy Prophet ﷺ said:

> The longest of you in qunūt in this world will be the most restful of you on the Day of Resurrection at the stand.[140]

---

139 Ṣadūq, Shaykh Muḥammad b. ʿAlī, *Man Lā Yaḥḍuruh al-Faqīh*, Vol. 1, p. 316.

140 Ṣadūq, Shaykh Muḥammad b. ʿAlī, *al-Amālī*, p. 509.

The prayers of the believers are ranked according to the level of perfection they embody and the proximity to their Lord through them. It is narrated that the Holy Prophet ﷺ has said:

> From between prayers, there are some from which what is accepted is its half, and its third, and its quarter, and its fifth up to the tenth. And some are wrapped like an old garment, and the face of its performer is struck with it. And for you from your prayer is what you have concentrated upon with your heart.[141]

One of the factors and causes of this blessing is for the worshipper to lengthen his qunūt, as is narrated from the Holy Prophet ﷺ, when he said:

> The best prayer is the one with a long qunūt.[142].

And so one can take the opportunity in qunūt to apologise to his Lord Almighty for his negligence in the first two rakʿahs of his prayer, and ask for assistance to complete what remains of his prayer.

One of the things that keeps believers awake at night is primarily the fear regarding their end, meaning the

---

[141] Majlisī, ʿAllāmah Muḥammad Bāqir, *Biḥār al-Anwār*, Vol. 81, p. 260.

[142] al-Ḥurr al-ʿĀmilī, Shaykh Muḥammad, *Wasāʾil al-Shīʿah*, Vol. 6, p. 292.

possibility of a bad outcome in the Hereafter. Then comes the fear of their final death throes, even if they end up with a good outcome in the Hereafter. There is no way to find out what can save us from these things except through those with knowledge of the secrets of creation, the Holy Prophet ﷺ and his Household ؑ, whom God ﷻ has informed of the unseen. The Holy Prophet has enlightened us with one of the things that brings respite on that ghastly day, where he says:

> Prolonging qunūt in prayer eases the throes of death.[143]

Prolonging the qunūt is just like prolonging any other act of worship; it starts difficult and challenging, but with enough repetition the soul starts to take pleasure in it, in addition to God's ﷻ intervention in attracting the souls of His faithful servants to acts of worship, as is understood from the Holy Verse:

﴿وَلَٰكِنَّ ٱللَّهَ حَبَّبَ إِلَيۡكُمُ ٱلۡإِيمَٰنَ وَزَيَّنَهُۥ فِي قُلُوبِكُمۡ﴾

﴾*wa-lākinna llāha ḥabbaba ilaykumu l-ʾīmāna wa-zayyanahū fī qulūbikum*﴿

﴾*But God has endeared faith to you and made it appealing in your hearts*﴿[144]

---

[143] al-Hindī, ʿAlī al-Muttaqī, *Kanz al-ʿUmmāl fī Sunan al-Aqwāl wal-Afʿāl*, Vol. 7, p. 435.

[144] Sūrat al-Ḥujurāt, Verse 7.

After such an intervention, the enjoyment of worship is not limited to prayer. Rather, the entire life of the servant turns into a place to enjoy that divine connection, as Imām Zayn al-ʿĀbidīn ﷺ describes by saying:

> O my bliss and my garden. O my world and my hereafter...[145]

The narrations indicate the two portions of qunūt. One of them involves the servant reciting anything that comes to mind. So he can begin by praising God ﷻ, requesting His blessings upon Ahl al-Bayt ﷺ and the reappearance of the Awaited Imām ﷺ, and then go on to request his needs for this world and the Hereafter. It is narrated that, when asked about what one should say in qunūt, Imām Jaʿfar aṣ-Ṣādiq ﷺ said:

> Whatever God makes to come out from your tongue.[146].

The other involves reciting the beautiful duʿāʾ that have been provided for us, as Imām Jaʿfar aṣ-Ṣādiq ﷺ said:

---

[145] Majlisī, ʿAllāmah Muḥammad Bāqir, *Biḥār al-Anwār*, Vol. 91, p. 142.

[146] Kulaynī, Shaykh Muḥammad b. Yaʿqūb, *al-Kāfī*, Vol. 3, p. 340.

> O Lord, forgive us, grant us mercy, good health, and pardon us in this world and in the next life; You have power over all things.[147]

There are occasions when qunūt is performed more than once in prayer. These are the times of Muslim gatherings, such as Friday Prayers or ʿĪd Prayers. Indeed, the accumulation of a large group of believers for a single purpose greatly contributes to attaining Divine fulfilment. It is narrated that Imām Jaʿfar aṣ-Ṣādiq ﵇ said:

> If a group of forty people come together to pray and plead before God, the Most Majestic, the Most Holy, for help in a matter, God will accept their prayers. If they are not forty, then four people can pray to God, the Most Majestic, the Most Holy, ten times and still God will accept their prayer.[148]

qunūt is one of the most important places to recite ṣalawāt, as it is a major component in fulfilling the obligation. By doing so, one starts his supplication by requesting blessings upon the Holy Prophet ﷺ and his Household ﵈, and according to our narrations, it is contrary to God's ﷻ mercy to answer the first and last requests of one's duʿā', and not the middle. Hence, the servant must definitely try to ask for as much forgiveness and as many needs as he can between those two guaranteed requests.

---

147 Ibid.

148 Ibid., Vol. 2, p. 487.

One of the greatest taʿqībāt one can perform after prayer is Tasbīḥat az-Zahrāʾ 🌸, one of the spiritual inheritances of this great lady that she was granted when she asked her father 🌸 for a maid. And so God 🌸 compensated her with this tasbīḥ, which is considered a divine treasure bestowed by God 🌸 upon the nation of her father 🌸 until the Day of Judgement. This is verified by what is narrated from Imām Muḥammad al-Bāqir 🌸:

> In worshipping God, in the form of praises, no other thing is better than tasbīḥ of Fāṭimah al-Zahrāʾ 🌸. If anything other than this could make a better gift, the Messenger of God would have instead given it to Fāṭimah al-Zahrāʾ 🌸.[149]

It seems that this rite's association with Sayyidah Fāṭimah 🌸 is what gave it this effect, as it is narrated that Imām Jaʿfar aṣ-Ṣādiq 🌸 said:

> Tasbīḥ of Fāṭimah al-Zahrāʾ 🌸 every day after every prayer is more beloved to me than one thousand rakʿah prayer every day.[150]

The true believer loves the turbah of Imām al-Ḥusayn 🌸 just as he loves who it belongs to. Just like prostrating on that blessed soil, holding a miṣbāḥ made from it has its own

---

[149] Ibid., p. 343.

[150] Ibid.

value, which is understood from the narration of Imām Jaʿfar aṣ-Ṣādiq ﷷ:

> Prostrating on the turbah of Imām al-Ḥusayn illuminates all seven earths, and one who were to have a rosary with him from clay of the grave of Imām al-Ḥusayn, he will be written as glorifying, even if he does not glorify with it[151].

And so it is fitting for one to recite Tasbīḥat az-Zahrāʾ ﷺ while grasping that blessed soil to be counted among those who praise God ﷻ, even if he forgets to praise God ﷻ after finishing from it. For it is narrated that Imām Jaʿfar aṣ-Ṣādiq ﷷ said:

> One who rotates the stones of the soil of Imām al-Ḥusayn seeking forgiveness with it one time, God ﷻ writes it for him seventy times, and if he holds the rosary in his hand and does not glorify with it, then in each bead from it is seven times.[152]

The worshipper is granted a special celestial privilege after every prayer: a guaranteed duʿāʾ. And the person who truly comprehends this fact cannot help but make a special interlude after prayer to have a heartfelt conversation with God ﷻ, carrying the special aura of prayer even after it

---

[151] al-Ḥurr al-ʿĀmilī, Shaykh Muḥammad, *Wasāʾil al-Shīʿah*, Vol. 5, p. 365.

[152] Ibid., Vol. 6, p. 456.

concludes, especially if it was a truly sincere prayer. Imām 'Alī ☙ has narrated that the Holy Prophet ﷺ once said:

> One who fulfils a prescribed prayer for God, for him would be an answer of a supplication in its tracks.[153]

Some of us may be satisfied with reciting only the well-known ta'qībāt after prayer, but what prevents us from enduring in a long and earnest conversation with God ﷻ? Especially if he finds within himself a special desire to have such a dialogue, choosing from the fifteen munaajayaat the one that suits his situation. By doing so, one can achieve a sense of sincerity in that munajaat that lasts even longer than that felt during prayer. In fact, it is narrated that he who follows his prayer with ta'qīb is, in reality, still in prayer. How beautiful it is for one to combine the rewards of the prayer with the blessings of the conversation with God ﷻ?

Some of our greatest scholars, specifically Sayyid Muḥammad Kāẓim al-Yazdī, known as Ṣāḥib al-'Urwah, define ta'qīb as:

> Busying oneself just after prayer with supplication, dhikr, Qur'ān recitation, or any other good deeds, like contemplating the glory of God ﷻ and such, or like weeping in fear of God ﷻ or gratitude and such. It seems it is also mustaḥabb after supplementary prayers,

---

[153] Ṭūsī, Shaykh Muḥammad b. Ḥasan, al-Amālī, p. 289.

> although it is more emphasized after wājib prayers. It is a condition that it be performed directly after finishing the prayer, without performing any other act that would void its form, which differs in different situations, such as travel and residency, urgency, and composure. For its form in travel, it may apply while riding or walking, just as it would in an urgent situation. The criterion for maintenance of the form is its application in the view of religious people. What is most certain in times of residency is that it applies to sitting, active, with what has been mentioned of supplication and the sort. And apparently, it does not apply while sitting without worship or while worshiping in a non-seated position, except in the aforementioned cases. And it is recommended to be facing the qiblah, in a state of cleanliness and ṭahārah, and in the presence of the place of prayer.[154]

Something that motivates the soul to be more focused in duʿāʾ is the belief in the existence of a correlation between all forms of livelihood and all forms of taʿqīb, for it is narrated that Imām Jaʿfar aṣ-Ṣādiq ﷺ said:

---

[154] al-Yazdī, Sayyid Muḥammad Kāẓim, *al-ʿUrwat al-Wuthqā*, Vol. 2, p. 615.

> The follow-up acts of worship are more extensive in seeking sustenance than the striking (for earning) in the land.[155]

Another source of abundant sustenance is to stay awake between twilight and sunrise, as it is mustaḥabb after praying Fajr to sit in the prayer place until sunrise, busying oneself with dhikr and praise of God ﷻ, as is narrated from Imām ʿAlī ؑ:

> Ask God for your share of daily sustenance from dawn until sunrise. This would be better than going around after work, since this is the time at which God divides his servants' share of daily livelihood.[156]

The upcoming day that the servant faces is filled with destinies that God ﷻ has written for him, some of which are punishments for negligence he has been guilty of in previous days. And so one of the blessings of morning taʿqībāt, one of them being istiʿādhah, is to push away these punishments, even if they seem irreversible, saying:

> I entrust to God the Exalted, the Lofty, my religion and myself, and my family, and my wealth, and my children, and my brothers in faith, and the entirety of what my

---

[155] al-Ḥurr al-ʿĀmilī, Shaykh Muḥammad, *Wasāʾil al-Shīʿah*, Vol. 6, p. 429.

[156] Ṣadūq, Shaykh Muḥammad b. ʿAlī, *al-Khiṣāl*, Vol. 2, p. 610.

> Lord has Graced me with, and the ends of my actions, and those whose affairs concern me...[157]

What is interesting here is that this istiʿādhah is so powerful in its protection against evil and misfortune that it shelters not only the servant himself, but also those around him, from his family and children to every believer he cares for.

The best gift one can give their brother in faith is one that helps them prepare for the Hereafter, such as a prayer kit. The more complete the kit is, the closer the meeting is to being accepted by God ﷻ. This is the same kit mentioned by Imām Mūsā al-Kāẓim ﵇, who said:

> The believer is not vacant from five: a toothbrush, a comb, a turbah, a rosary wherein are thirty-four beads, and a ring of ʿaqīq.[158]

The believer is told to be in a constant state of contemplation, as it is narrated that:

> Contemplating for one hour is better than worshipping a whole night.[159]

---

157 *al-Balad al-Amīn*, Vol. 1, p. 9.

158 al-Ḥurr al-ʿĀmilī, Shaykh Muḥammad, *Wasāʾil al-Shīʿah*, Vol. 6, p. 456.

159 Kulaynī, Shaykh Muḥammad b. Yaʿqūb, *al-Kāfī*, Vol. 2, p. 54.

And some of the best times for contemplation are just after Fajr and Maghrib prayers. Those are the times at which the heart is at rest and ease, for the person has finished from the bustle of life, and all its disturbances. Now is the time to contemplate the previous day, what he spent it doing, and what he must achieve tomorrow. In fact, he should revise his entire life trajectory to know where he has reached in his preparation for death and how ready he is to defend himself in the grand court of the Almighty Lord!

# The Inner Etiquettes of Ṣalāt al-Layl

Ṣalāt al-Layl[160] and jamāʿah prayers are both mustaḥabb acts of worship, but of different colours. The former is performed in the secrecy of the night, while the latter is performed in a public gathering of people. But he who has accustomed himself to standing before his Almighty Lord alone in the middle of the night will find himself safe from the trap of riyāʾ when he prays jamāʿah in front of many people. For he is, in both cases, in an appointment with Him whom he has amplified in his heart, shrinking everything else other than Him.

When the Holy Prophet ﷺ urged Imām ʿAlī ؑ to pray Ṣalāt al-Layl, he asked God ﷻ to aid him in performing it, saying:

> O Ali, I hereby bequeath to you qualities, so preserve them from me. Then he said:
>
> > O God, Support him,
>
> Until he said:
>
> > And it is on you to perform the Night Prayer, and it is on you to perform the Night Prayer, and it is on you to perform the Night Prayer.[161]

---

[160] Also known as *Qiyām al-Layl*, or *Tahajjud*.

[161] al-Ḥurr al-ʿĀmilī, Shaykh Muḥammad, *Wasāʾil al-Shīʿah*, Vol. 5, p. 181.

And perhaps the secret in that lies in the Holy Prophet ﷺ's knowledge of the difficult times he will go through, such as the night of Ḥarīr. Or perhaps it was the Holy Prophet ﷺ's expectations of his successor to be in the highest form of dedication to it, to emulate his own state during Ṣalāt al-Layl, as he describes himself:

> I have states with God ﷻ, unbearable to a close angel, or a sent messenger.[162]

It is narrated that Imām al-Ḥasan al-ʿAskarī ؑ has said:

> Arriving at God, Mighty and Majestic, is a journey. It cannot be realised except by 'riding' the night.[163]

meaning that this strenuous journey is made easier only by riding a particular vehicle, and that vehicle is Qiyām al-Layl. And although night prayers may seem challenging for those who have not experienced and enjoyed them, the desired objective, to reach God ﷻ, is itself an incentive above any other possible incentive. It should also be known that in the entire history of faithful believers and pious servants, not once has any of them reached where they did without being one of the 'people of the night'.

---

162 Narāqī, Muḥaqqiq, *Jāmiʿ al-Saʿādāt*, Vol. 1, p. 45.

163 Majlisī, ʿAllāmah Muḥammad Bāqir, *Biḥār al-Anwār*, Vol. 75, p. 380.

The Noble Qur'ān has mentioned the reward for tahajjud, though somewhat ambiguously, in the Holy Verse:

﴿وَمِنَ ٱلَّيْلِ فَتَهَجَّدْ بِهِۦ نَافِلَةً لَّكَ عَسَىٰٓ أَن يَبْعَثَكَ رَبُّكَ مَقَامًا مَّحْمُودًا﴾

*﴿wa-mina l-layli fa-tahajjad bihī nāfilatan laka ʿasā an yabʿathaka rabbuka maqāman maḥmūdan﴾*

*﴿And keep vigil for a part of the night, as a supererogatory [devotion] for you. It may be that your Lord will raise you to a praiseworthy station﴾*[164]

whereas the Noble Qur'ān has always specified the reward for different acts of worship, as motivation for the worshippers. So perhaps the ambiguity here stems from the fact that the rewards are indescribable or incommunicable. God's ﷻ bestowments upon his servants in the dead of night are something that can only be realised, not described, rendering it out of reach of the comprehension of those who have not savoured such rewards. It could also derive from the fact that God ﷻ does not want to mention the prize of solitude with Him. This is supported by what Imām Jaʿfar aṣ-Ṣādiq ؑ says:

> There is no good deed the servant does except there is a reward (mentioned) in the Qur'ān, except the night

[164] Sūrat al-Isrā', Verse 79.

> Ṣalāt, for God did not state its rewards due to the largeness of its size to Him.[165]

The mention of the prize of a specific act of worship in the narrations means that, by performing that act, the servant deserves that reward, not that that reward is automatically granted. The worshipper should not expect to receive that reward by simply performing that act for a short period of time, for perhaps there is a condition he has missed, or something that prevents that reward from reaching him. It is for this reason that the Holy Verse aforementioned did not guarantee the gratification of the 'praiseworthy station'; rather, it mentioned it in the context of anticipation, using the word 'may' so that the servant does not depend completely on his worship. For the entry to the 'praiseworthy station' has its own equation that the human brain does not understand, and can only be comprehended by the Knowing and Aware.

If the servant accomplishes all of his duties and performs all of the acts of worship possible, but does not perform Qiyām al-Layl, he will remain incomplete. Even if he is a soldier for the sake of God ﷻ, or the biggest donor for His cause, for it is narrated that Imām Ja'far aṣ-Ṣādiq ؑ said:

---

165 al-Ḥurr al-'Āmilī, Shaykh Muḥammad, *Wasā'il al-Shī'ah*, Vol. 8, p. 163.

> The nobility of a man is in his prayer during the night.[166].

Indeed, this nobility has a great influence in the Hereafter, for the nobles' sector in Heaven is only entered by 'the people of the night'.

There is a correlation between sustenance, both material and spiritual, and Qiyām al-Layl, for it is narrated that Imām Jaʿfar aṣ-Ṣādiq ﷺ said:

> The night Ṣalāt guarantees sustenance at daytime.[167]

As it has been narrated:

> A man commits sins, and he is deprived of the prayer at night.[168]

Sin prevents one from performing Ṣalāt al-Layl, and ultimately blocks all and any blessings from reaching the servant. Realising this greatly motivates one to commit himself to Qiyām al-Layl, and there is no doubt that one adapts to his internal motivations, for a body will not weaken from what the intention has strengthened upon. Indeed, the promise of great rewards, valuable knowledge,

---

166 Kulaynī, Shaykh Muḥammad b. Yaʿqūb, *al-Kāfī*, Vol. 3, p. 488.

167 al-Ḥurr al-ʿĀmilī, Shaykh Muḥammad, *Wasāʾil al-Shīʿah*, Vol. 8, p. 158.

168 Kulaynī, Shaykh Muḥammad b. Yaʿqūb, *al-Kāfī*, Vol. 2, p. 272.

a fruitful charity, a respectful wife, prosperous offspring, and much more will surely create that unwavering determination in the soul.

Inability to devote oneself to Ṣalāt al-Layl is in itself a huge loss, but it also exposes a flaw and weakness in the soul that has caused this deprivation. Hence, the believer should not neglect this blunder, and should instead look for its roots, to ensure it will not occur again the next night, for every day and night has its own separate judgement. So negligence on that day resulted in deprivation that night. A person once approached Imām ʿAlī ﷺ, bemoaning his deprivation, to which the Healer of the Souls revealed the ailment, saying,

> Your sins enslave you.[169]

Dedication to performing the mustaḥabbbaat is a condition of attaining the fruits of worship. One who performs acts of worship depending on his mood, or gives them a try on some days and nights, cannot expect to gain the rewards for them mentioned in the Noble Qurʾān or the narrations. If one wishes to be counted among those 'repentant in the dead of night', he must commit to reciting istighfār during Ṣalāt al-Layl for an entire year, for it is narrated that Imām Muḥammad al-Bāqir ﷺ said:

---

[169] *at-Tawḥīd*, p. 97.

> One who is constant upon the night Ṣalāt and al-Witr and seeks forgiveness of God ﷻ seventy times during every Witr, then persists upon that for a year, will be written as being from the ones seeking forgiveness at pre-dawn.[170]

Even if he is later denied this privilege, he will remain characterised by that blessed trait. How glorious it is that one can attain this honor by regulating oneself for a single year!

The persistent invitation to Qiyām al-Layl is not directed to a specific portion of people; rather, it involves the best of the nation, the same people the Holy Prophet ﷺ meant when he said:

> Jibrā'īl has not ceased to advise me to stand at night until I thought that the best of my community will not sleep.[171].

How embarrassing it is for God ﷻ to watch over the people of a society, finding some who do not follow the path of Ahl al-Bayt ﷺ and still pray Ṣalāt al-Layl, while others who claim to follow Ahl al-Bayt ﷺ are ignorant and asleep at

---

170 Majlisī, 'Allāmah Muḥammad Bāqir, *Biḥār al-Anwār*, Vol. 84, p. 225.

171 al-Ḥurr al-'Āmilī, Shaykh Muḥammad, *Wasā'il al-Shī'ah*, Vol. 8, p. 154.

night! Imām Jaʿfar aṣ-Ṣādiq 🕮 reproachfully excludes such people from those close to Ahl al-Bayt 🕮 when he says:

> He is not from us, one who does not pray the Night Prayer.[172]

The light that flows between the hands of the believers of the Day of Judgement, as the Noble Qurʾān describes, also touches the hearts of the night worshippers, such that it illuminates their faces in this world, even if those without vision do not observe it. Imām Zayn al-ʿĀbidīn 🕮 was once asked:

> What is the matter that the diligent ones at night are from the people with the best of faces? He said: Because they are alone with God, so God drapes them from His light.[173]

Indeed, this glow has its effects even in this world: a beauty in their speech, a charm in their appearance, and an effect on the souls of others, and it is the meaning of endearment which God 🕮 pledged to grant to His devotees.

The believer has two checkpoints a day to purify his interior from the stains of sin that have stuck to it over time: A checkpoint during the day, istighfār after ʿAṣr prayer, for Imām Jaʿfar aṣ-Ṣādiq 🕮 is narrated to have said:

---

[172] Ibid., p. 162.

[173] Ṣadūq, Shaykh Muḥammad b. ʿAlī, *ʿIlal al-Sharāiʿ*, Vol. 2, p. 365.

> Whoever repents to God seventy times after ʿAṣr, God forgives seven hundred sins that day from him.[174]

And another checkpoint at night, istighfār in the Witr prayer seventy times, which is narrated to have its effect in absolution from wrongdoings, as Imām Jaʿfar aṣ-Ṣādiq ﷺ also says:

> The prayer of a believing person during the night eliminates the bad deeds he has done during the day.[175]

One of the toughest stages on the Day of Judgement is the stage of compensation to the people. For God ﷻ may forgive what has to do with His rights, but the people's rights are left to them to forgive each other. And it is here that the value of istighfār shows itself to the worshippers of the night, for this night, repentance might be what is needed to make an oppressed servant forgive his oppressor, for it is akin to conserved credit that reveals its usefulness on that strenuous day.

Some people, out of laziness, skip Ṣalāt al-Layl entirely, missing all its rakʿahs. But where is the problem in committing oneself to the bare minimum of Qiyām, like praying only Shafʿ and Witr, even if before midnight—for those allowed to—at least until he feels the blessings of his

---

[174] al-Ḥurr al-ʿĀmilī, Shaykh Muḥammad, *Wasā'il al-Shīʿah*, Vol. 6, p. 482.

[175] Kulaynī, Shaykh Muḥammad b. Yaʿqūb, *al-Kāfī*, Vol. 3, p. 266.

worship, inviting him for more? And this little that the servant commits to is something that brings the compassion of God ﷻ, for it is narrated that Imām Muḥammad al-Bāqir ؑ said:

> The most beloved of deeds in the sight of God, most Majestic, most Glorious, is that which a servant continues even if it is very little.[176]

There are some things advised for those who wish to perform Ṣalāt al-Layl but are concerned that sleep will overcome them. These include:

Reciting the last verse of Sūrat al-Kahf:

﴿قُلْ إِنَّمَآ أَنَا۠ بَشَرٌ مِّثْلُكُمْ يُوحَىٰٓ إِلَيَّ أَنَّمَآ إِلَٰهُكُمْ إِلَٰهٌ وَٰحِدٌ ۖ فَمَن كَانَ يَرْجُوا۟ لِقَآءَ رَبِّهِۦ فَلْيَعْمَلْ عَمَلًا صَٰلِحًا وَلَا يُشْرِكْ بِعِبَادَةِ رَبِّهِۦٓ أَحَدًۢا﴾

*﴿qul innamā ana basharun mithlukum yūḥā ilayya annamā ilāhukum ilāhun wāḥidun fa-man kāna yarjū liqā'a rabbihī fa-l-ya'mal 'amalan ṣāliḥan wa-lā yushrik bi-'ibādati rabbihī aḥadan﴾*

*﴿Say, 'I am just a human being like you. It has been revealed to me that your God is the One God. So whoever expects to*

[176] Ibid., Vol. 2, p. 82.

*encounter his Lord—let him act righteously, and not associate anyone with the worship of his Lord*﴿[177]

Āyat al-Kursī three times:

﴿ٱللَّهُ لَآ إِلَٰهَ إِلَّا هُوَ ٱلْحَيُّ ٱلْقَيُّومُۚ لَا تَأْخُذُهُۥ سِنَةٌ وَلَا نَوْمٌۚ لَّهُۥ مَا فِي ٱلسَّمَٰوَٰتِ وَمَا فِي ٱلْأَرْضِۗ مَن ذَا ٱلَّذِي يَشْفَعُ عِندَهُۥٓ إِلَّا بِإِذْنِهِۦۚ يَعْلَمُ مَا بَيْنَ أَيْدِيهِمْ وَمَا خَلْفَهُمْۖ وَلَا يُحِيطُونَ بِشَيْءٍ مِّنْ عِلْمِهِۦٓ إِلَّا بِمَا شَآءَۚ وَسِعَ كُرْسِيُّهُ ٱلسَّمَٰوَٰتِ وَٱلْأَرْضَۖ وَلَا يَـُٔودُهُۥ حِفْظُهُمَاۚ وَهُوَ ٱلْعَلِيُّ ٱلْعَظِيمُ﴾

﴾*allāhu lā ilāha illā huwa l-ḥayyu l-qayyūmu lā ta'khudhuhū sinatun wa-lā nawmun lahū mā fī s-samāwāti wa-mā fī l-'arḍi man dhā lladhī yashfa'u 'indahū illā bi-'idhnihī ya'lamu mā bayna aydīhim wa-mā khalfahum wa-lā yuḥīṭūna bi-shay'in min 'ilmihī illā bi-mā shā'a wasi'a kursiyyuhu s-samāwāti wa-l-'arḍa wa-lā ya'ūduhū ḥifẓuhumā wa-huwa l-'aliyyu l-'aẓīmu*﴿

﴾*God—there is no god except Him—is the Living One, the Sustainer. Neither drowsiness befalls Him nor sleep. To Him belongs whatever is in the heavens and whatever is on the earth. Who is it that may intercede with Him except with His permission? He knows what is before them and what is behind them, and they do not comprehend anything of His knowledge except what He wishes. His seat embraces the*

---

177 Sūrat al-Kahf, Verse 110.

*heavens and the earth and He is not wearied by their preservation, and He is the Exalted, the Supreme*﴿[178]

the verse

﴿شَهِدَ ٱللَّهُ أَنَّهُۥ لَآ إِلَٰهَ إِلَّا هُوَ وَٱلۡمَلَٰٓئِكَةُ وَأُوْلُواْ ٱلۡعِلۡمِ قَآئِمَۢا بِٱلۡقِسۡطِۚ لَآ إِلَٰهَ إِلَّا هُوَ ٱلۡعَزِيزُ ٱلۡحَكِيمُ﴾

﴾*shahida llāhu annahū lā ilāha illā huwa wa-l-malā'ikatu wa-'ulū l-'ilmi qā'iman bi-l-qisṭi lā ilāha illā huwa l-'azīzu l-ḥakīm*[u]﴿

﴾*God, maintainer of justice, the Almighty and the Wise, besides whom there is no god, bears witness that there is no god except Him, and [so do] the angels and those who possess knowledge*﴿[179]

Āyāt al-Sukhrah:

﴿إِنَّ رَبَّكُمُ ٱللَّهُ ٱلَّذِي خَلَقَ ٱلسَّمَٰوَٰتِ وَٱلۡأَرۡضَ فِي سِتَّةِ أَيَّامٖ ثُمَّ ٱسۡتَوَىٰ عَلَى ٱلۡعَرۡشِۖ يُغۡشِي ٱلَّيۡلَ ٱلنَّهَارَ يَطۡلُبُهُۥ حَثِيثٗا وَٱلشَّمۡسَ وَٱلۡقَمَرَ وَٱلنُّجُومَ مُسَخَّرَٰتِۭ بِأَمۡرِهِۦٓۗ أَلَا لَهُ ٱلۡخَلۡقُ وَٱلۡأَمۡرُۗ تَبَارَكَ ٱللَّهُ رَبُّ ٱلۡعَٰلَمِينَ﴾

---

[178] Sūrat al-Baqarah, Verse 255.

[179] Sūrat Āl 'Imrān, Verse 18.

﴾*inna rabbakumu llāhu lladhī khalaqa s-samāwāti wa-l-'arḍa fī sittati ayyāmin thumma stawā 'alā l-'arshi yughshī l-layla n-nahāra yaṭlubuhū ḥathīthan wa-sh-shamsa wa-l-qamara wa-n-nujūma musakhkharātin bi-'amrihī a-lā lahu l-khalqu wa-l-'amru tabāraka llāhu rabbu l-'ālamīn*[a]﴿

﴾ٱدْعُوا۟ رَبَّكُمْ تَضَرُّعًا وَخُفْيَةً ۚ إِنَّهُۥ لَا يُحِبُّ ٱلْمُعْتَدِينَ﴿

﴾*ud'ū rabbakum taḍarru'an wa-khufyatan innahū lā yuḥibbu l-mu'tadīn*[a]﴿

﴾وَلَا تُفْسِدُوا۟ فِى ٱلْأَرْضِ بَعْدَ إِصْلَـٰحِهَا وَٱدْعُوهُ خَوْفًا وَطَمَعًا ۚ إِنَّ رَحْمَتَ ٱللَّهِ قَرِيبٌ مِّنَ ٱلْمُحْسِنِينَ﴿

﴾*wa-lā tufsidū fī l-'arḍi ba'da iṣlāḥihā wa-d'ūhu khawfan wa-ṭama'an inna raḥmata llāhi qarībun mina l-muḥsinīn*[a]﴿

﴾*Indeed your Lord is God, who created the heavens and the earth in six days, and then settled on the Throne. He draws the night's cover over the day, which pursues it swiftly, and [He created] the sun, the moon, and the stars, [all of them] disposed by His command. Look! All creation and command belong to Him. Blessed is God, the Lord of all the worlds. Supplicate your Lord, beseechingly and secretly. Indeed, He does not like the transgressors. And do not cause corruption on the earth after its restoration, and supplicate Him with fear and hope: indeed God's mercy is close to the virtuous*﴿[180]

Reciting Tasbīḥat az-Zahrā' ﷺ, and sleeping with wuḍū'.

Reciting what has been advised by the Holy Prophet ﷺ:

> Whoever likes to wake up at night, at the time of going to sleep should say,
>
> > O Lord, do not allow me to ignore Your anger, do not allow me to forget speaking of You, do not make me of the careless ones, so I will wake up at such and such hour,
>
> God, the Most Majestic, the Most Holy, will assign an angel to wake him up at that time[181]

Thanking God ﷻ for the blessing of awakening when the servant leaves his bed, for it is narrated that Imām Muḥammad al-Bāqir ؑ said:

> During the night if you wake up, say,

[180] Sūrat al-A'rāf, Verses 54–56.

[181] Kulaynī, Shaykh Muḥammad b. Ya'qūb, *al-Kāfī*, Vol. 2, p. 540.

> All praise belongs to God, who has returned my spirit to me so I can thank Him and worship Him.[182]

Eating a light dinner; a heavy dinner causes heavy sleep.

Sleeping early, as the fatigued body that has not had enough rest will not respond to its owner with any form of energy or enthusiasm.

Having that spiritual motivation before sleep, feeling a sense of worry for the possibility of missing tahajjud that night, and missing out on gaining proximity to God ﷻ.

One of the blessings exclusive to the people of Qiyām al-Layl and Fajr prayer is their presence in the assembly time of both the ascending night angels and the descending morning angels. And that is what is meant by the Noble Qur'ān when it says:

﴿إِنَّ قُرْءَانَ ٱلْفَجْرِ كَانَ مَشْهُودًا﴾

﴾*inna qur'āna l-fajri kāna mashhūdaⁿ*﴿

﴾*Indeed the dawn recital is attended [by angels]*﴿[183]

[182] Ibid., Vol. 3, p. 445.

[183] Sūrat al-Isrā', Verse 78.

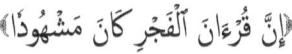

And there is no doubt that the testimony of two kinds of angels in favour of the loyal servants in this hour is an acknowledged testimony to God ﷻ. It should also be known that these angels are given the job of judging the servants by God ﷻ, and also ask for forgiveness for those on Earth.

There is a certain verse in the Noble Qur'ān that, should the servant truly contemplate it, he would become fearful of being one of those mentioned in it, for it talks about a situation in which God ﷻ dislikes the good from His servant. So He weakens him and causes him to waver from that obedience. That is the Holy Verse:

﴿وَلَٰكِن كَرِهَ ٱللَّهُ ٱنۢبِعَاثَهُمۡ فَثَبَّطَهُمۡ وَقِيلَ ٱقۡعُدُواْ مَعَ ٱلۡقَٰعِدِينَ﴾

﴾*wa-lākin kariha llāhu nbi'āthahum fa-thabbaṭahum wa-qīla q'udū ma'a l-qā'idīn[a]*﴿

﴾*but God was averse to arouse them, so He held them back, and it was said [to them], 'Be seated with those who sit back.'*﴿[184]

Even though the Verse was revealed in the context of Jihad, it is still very possible for God ﷻ to weaken His servant from good deeds in other situations, and that is when He wants to abandon the person. An example of this is in Ṣalāt al-Layl, where a person would wake up at night intending

[184] Sūrat at-Tawbah, Verse 46.

to do something beyond just Fajr prayer, but would not find himself yearning for Qiyām al-Layl.

There is no doubt that the simple act of waking up at night with the intention of praying Ṣalāt al-Layl, forsaking his own rest, in itself brings upon the servant God's ﷻ merciful gaze for what he struggles through when 'his side leaves his bed', as described by the Noble Qur'ān. So imagine if the prayer were bolstered by sincerity and desire. The servant could be performing his prayers while swaying left and right from tiredness, and yet God ﷻ would proudly brag about him to His angels. It is narrated from Imām Jaʿfar aṣ-Ṣādiq (ع) that God ﷻ says:

> Look at My servant, what he is going through to be closer to Me with what I did not obligate upon him.[185]

One of the striking scenes for those in the sky is the sight of a faithful couple upholding Qiyām al-Layl, each reminding the other. It is narrated that the Holy Prophet ﷺ said:

> May God have mercy on a man who gets up at night and prays, and awakens his wife; if she refuses, he should sprinkle water on her face. May God have mercy on a woman who gets up at night and prays, and

185 Ṣadūq, Shaykh Muḥammad b. ʿAlī, *ʿIlal al-Sharāiʿ*, Vol. 2, p. 364.

> awakens her husband; if he refuses, she would sprinkle water on his face.[186]

The result is a family that transforms into something akin to a shining star in the skies. That couple is written among those who remember God ﷻ constantly, even if their remembrance wanes after that. And you can imagine the array of blessings landing on that house filled with recital of the Noble Qur'ān, and prayer before God ﷻ!

If the veil were to be removed from the eyes of a servant praying at night—in a secluded, unadulterated solitude—he would see a breathtaking number of angels surrounding him. And if it were not for the narrations of Ahl al-Bayt (ع) revealing these facts to us, we would have never comprehended them, and they would have remained elusive to us. And here we say: what prevents the servant from greeting this gathering of angels encompassing him in the dead of night? This is understood from the narration of the Holy Prophet ﷺ, the master of the night worshippers:

> Whichever male or female servant is granted a night prayer, standing purified before God, washing thoroughly in ablution, praying for God with an honest intention, a peaceable heart, a body in awe, and a tearful eye, God will put nine rows of angels behind him—the number in each row is not known to anyone

[186] al-Sijistānī, Abū Dāwūd, *Sunan Abī Dāwūd*, The Book of Prayer, Vol. 2, p. 33.

except God—one end of the row will be in the East, and the other in the West. He said:

> Once he finishes, he will be given ranks by their number.[187]

One of the biggest obstacles in the path of those seeking God ﷻ is the ambiguity of the terrain to them, such that they do not see how it is in reality. And so they are forced to experiment repetitively until they reach the objective, which they don't always do. He may be safe in terms of jurisprudential laws, for he follows what his scholar tells him to do. But the problem lies in scenarios that don't fall under any of those laws and therefore cannot be determined to be advisable or not. Here comes the role of the Divine light to show one how things really are. Something that shines this light into the heart of the believer is his devotion to Qiyām al-Layl, specifically the servant's isolation with his Almighty Lord, who does not refuse such a request after His servant's pleas.

It is well-known to the lovers of this finite world that nighttime is the time to have fun with their associates, without ever getting bored or tired, for time flies when they are deep in their pleasure. So how about those in the dead of night who have seen phenomena that bring shock at times, amazement at others, and sometimes even fear?! Therefore, we can consider the servant's abandonment of

---

[187] Ṣadūq, Shaykh Muḥammad b. ʿAlī, *al-Amālī*, p. 68.

his bed, impatient to meet his Lord, as a sign of his devotion and love for his life of servitude. It is narrated in a qudsī narration that:

> O son of 'Imrān! One who alleges that he loves Me yet sleeps away from Me when night befalls him has lied. Doesn't every lover love to be alone with his beloved?[188]

One of the times in which the servant is closest to his Lord is when he is prostrate. Another one of these times is the hour of Qiyām al-Layl. It is a designation separate but equivalent to that of sujūd, and his status and proximity to his Lord, should the veiled be uncovered to him, is the same as that in sujūd. And should he know before Whom he stands, and the mercy in store for him, he would never wish to leave his current position. And that is what we learn from the answer of Imām Ja'far aṣ-Ṣādiq ﷺ to those who asked him:

> Which time does the servant happen to be closest to God and God is close to him? He said: 'When he stands at the end of the night while his eyes are calm, he walks to his wuḍū' until he performs wuḍū' with a perfect wuḍū', then he comes until he stands in his praying place and faces his face to God, and lines his

---

188 al-Ḥurr al-'Āmilī, Shaykh Muḥammad, *Wasā'il al-Shī'ah*, Vol. 7, p. 77.

> feet, and raises his voice and exclaims in takbir and begins the prayer.[189]

One of the signs of the servant's misfortune is for him to be disregarded and detested by his Lord, and that is when he turns into a corpse at night. What is the difference between somebody asleep, negligent of remembering God ﷻ, and a dead human or animal?! The former is dead in the heart, warranting reproach and reproval, while the latter is physically dead, not deserving of any such blame. Imagining such a revolting prospect makes the servant work to turn his own sleep into worship by cleansing himself, reciting supplications, and then sleeping with the intention of waking up for Ṣalāt al-Layl. It is narrated that Prophet Mūsā ؑ asked:

> Oh Lord! Which of Your servants is most detested to You?

God ﷻ replied:

> A corpse at night, idle at daytime.[190]

God ﷻ has given His worshippers the option of making their night prayers as long or as brief as they wish, depending on their energy and spiritual appetite. And so

---

[189] Majlisī, ʿAllāmah Muḥammad Bāqir, *Biḥār al-Anwār*, Vol. 84, p. 158.

[190] Ibid., Vol. 13, p. 354.

one can perform all eleven rak'ahs, or make do with just Shaf' and Witr. The worshipper can also choose not to recite a Sūrah during a rak'ah, or he can recite multiple Sūrahs in a single rak'ah. He can perform Ṣalāt al-Layl before midnight—if his scholar allows so—and he can pray it Qaḍā' if he misses it. He can choose to pray it standing or sitting. He can skip the Qunūt, just as he can recite istighfār for forty believers, repeat the istighfār seventy times, then ask for forgiveness three hundred times. All of this in addition to the long supplications we are advised to recite before dawn.

Some of us think that concealing our wealth is always advisable, whereas in reality, the Noble Qur'ān describes the faithful as charitable in both secret and public. Giving in public, without riyā', encourages others to do the same. From here, we can also say that mentioning one's worship at night to others can be advisable if it serves a purpose that pleases God ﷻ, such as making it easier for others by emphasizing its simplicity, or motivating them by discussing its long-term and short-term benefits. It is narrated that Imām Muḥammad al-Bāqir ؑ said:

> There is no problem in discussing with your brother when you are hoping that it would benefit him and encourage him; and when he asks you,
>
> Did you stand for prayer at night, or fast?

Then narrate to him about that when you have done it, and say,

> God ﷻ has provided that,

And do not say,

> No.

For that would be a lie.[191]

[191] Ṭabrisī, Mīrzā Ḥusayn Nūrī, *Mustadrak al-Wasā'il wa-Mustanbaṭ al-Masā'il*, Vol. 1, p. 115.

# The Inner Etiquettes of the Mosque

The Noble Qur'ān is God's ﷻ communication with the servant, while prayer is the servant's communication with God ﷻ. For he who wishes to hear his Lord's words reads the Noble Qur'ān, and he who wishes to speak to his Lord prays to Him. And so, when present in the mosque, the believer is combining both of these lights. Therefore, can it not be said that sitting in the mosque is lovelier than sitting in Heaven?! This is what Imām ʿAlī ؑ said in the narration:

> Sitting in the mosque is better for me than sitting in Paradise, for in Paradise is my own satisfaction, while in the mosque is my Lord's satisfaction.[192]

God ﷻ has two types of commands: those to be performed in public and those to be performed in solitude. Sometimes we are told to pursue prayer in jamāʿah, or to perform Ḥajj or ʿĪd prayers, all of which are public acts. Other times, we are told to fast, pray Ṣalāt al-Layl, or give charity, all of which are done privately. And so God ﷻ wishes to be worshipped openly just as He wishes to be worshipped secretly. And those who perfect secret worship will not find trouble in open worship, so blessed is he who has a meeting with his Lord by night, and dialogue with him by day. Our souls require jamāʿah prayers in their paths towards perfection, just as they need Ṣalāt al-Layl, to emulate what we recite in Munājāt Shaʿbāniyyah:

---

192 al-Ḥurr al-ʿĀmilī, Shaykh Muḥammad, *Wasāʾil al-Shīʿah*, Vol. 5, p. 199.

> So You speak to him secretly, and he works for You openly.[193]

Truly fortunate is he who can combine both forms of worship in Fajr prayer, praying it in jamāʿah publicly, while walking to the mosque in the solitude of the night!

The believer should test the true extent of his faith by observing his condition in the mosque; should he find himself yearning to go to the mosque, that would be a sign that his Imaan is true. Another sign is that he finds himself looking forward to the next prayer, ultimately discovering a truth about himself: he enjoys being in the mosque more than he enjoys being in his house with his family. And so he follows one prayer with another and is among the first to enter the mosque, proving his love for it. It is narrated that Imām Jaʿfar aṣ-Ṣādiq ﵇ said:

> Three are from the pure servants of God ﷻ on the Day of Judgement:... and a man who enters the mosque, so he prays, and follows up with acts of worship waiting for the next prayer, and so he is a guest of God ﷻ, and it is a right upon God ﷻ to honor His guest.[194]

The servant must follow the proper etiquette when entering the mosque, through reciting the narrated

---

[193] Majlisī, ʿAllāmah Muḥammad Bāqir, *Biḥār al-Anwār*, Vol. 91, p. 96.

[194] al-Ḥurr al-ʿĀmilī, Shaykh Muḥammad, *Wasāʾil al-Shīʿah*, Vol. 4, p. 116.

supplications, entering with his right foot, leaving with his left foot, adorning himself, applying perfume, only entering with the cleanest and tidiest of clothes, and fully grasping that this place is the true, untainted property of God ﷻ. That feeling that he is in the house of God ﷻ and His accommodation certainly aids in observing all the formalities. And so, when he enters the mosque, he should invoke in himself the realisation that he is in a spot that belongs exclusively to God ﷻ.

The Imāms of Ahl al-Bayt عليهم السلام have been known to release their servants when they see in them an act of kindness or an apology, for being released is the ultimate wish of every servant. And there is no doubt that being released from Hellfire is more important than being released from apparent slavery. That is what is anticipated from the Owner of the mosque, for the servant enters the mosque begging for his neck to be freed from the punishment of Hellfire! And if that fateful salvation is anticipated from a single visit to the mosque, what is to be expected from recurring visits?!

Everybody who enters the Sacred Mosque in Makkah, the Mosque of the Holy Prophet ﷺ in Madīnah, or the sites of his Progeny عليهم السلام sheds his official identity and adorns himself in the attire of God's ﷻ hospitality. And that is the case for whoever enters the mosque, too, for he is now the guest of God ﷻ. Therefore, humiliating any worshipper in the mosque can bring about the anger of the Vengeful Lord, for that worshipper is under His protection and accommodation. Additionally, a person's commitment to attending the mosque leaves a good impression on people, making them comfortable with befriending him, performing exchanges with him, or even marrying him into their family, as is narrated from the Holy Prophet ﷺ:

> If one performs the five prayers in congregation, you should think well of him.[195]

There is no doubt that God's ﷻ companionship with the servant is constant, wherever he goes. But His presence is more intense at certain times, sometimes reaching a point at which the servant is labelled as God's ﷻ guest or invitee, living under the canopy of His mercy, as described in the Holy Verse:

﴿إِنَّ ٱللَّهَ مَعَ ٱلَّذِينَ ٱتَّقَوا۟ وَّٱلَّذِينَ هُم مُّحْسِنُونَ﴾

*﴾inna llāha maʿa lladhīna ttaqaw wa-lladhīna hum muḥsinūna[a]﴿*

*﴾Indeed God is with those who are Godwary and those who are virtuous﴿*[196]

And one of the acts that causes one to be in God's ﷻ hospitality, and be 'with' Him, is attending the mosque and praying in it.

---

[195] Ibid., Vol. 8, p. 286.

[196] Sūrat an-Naḥl, Verse 128.

Everywhere has its own etiquette and policies. The kings of this world stress proper decorum when meeting them, to the point that one is scared to overlook the rituals demanded of them. So what if He who he is going to meet is the Possessor of creation?! Therefore, one must strive to be at the utmost level of respect and veneration for God ﷻ, avoiding angering Him by disobeying Him in His sanctuary, and being polite in all his movements and actions when presenting his requests in His court. And so, our scholars have listed some behaviours that are makrūh to perform in the mosque.

Some may feel guilty about being unable to build a mosque for God ﷻ to be remembered in, and therefore build themselves a house in Heaven. But it is not required to build an entire mosque; rather, one only needs to erect what can generally be classified as one, even if very simple. It is narrated that Imām Muḥammad al-Bāqir ؑ has said:

> One who builds a mosque, and even if it were like the nest of a grouse, God ﷻ will build a house for him in Paradise.

Abū ʿUbaydah said,

> Abū Jaʿfar passed by me while I was between Makkah and Madīnah, and I was placing the rocks. I said,

> > This is from that?

He said:

> Yes.[197]

It is advised that the servant should follow the recommended manners in all circumstances, when using the washroom, performing wuḍū', prayer, Ghusl, eating and drinking, sleeping, riding a vehicle, donning his clothes, and all other daily actions. And the servant who watches himself carefully must follow what the Holy Prophet ﷺ would do when entering the mosque, where he would say:

> In the Name of God, and the greeting be unto the Holy Prophet. And when leaving, he would say: O God! Forgive me and open doors of Your grace for me![198]

To be counted as serving in the mosque, it is sufficient to do what the mother of Maryam ﷺ did, by asking God ﷻ to make her offspring a servant in Jerusalem (Bayt al-Maqdis), saying:

﴿إِذْ قَالَتِ ٱمْرَأَتُ عِمْرَٰنَ رَبِّ إِنِّي نَذَرْتُ لَكَ مَا فِي بَطْنِي مُحَرَّرًا فَتَقَبَّلْ مِنِّيٓ إِنَّكَ أَنتَ ٱلسَّمِيعُ ٱلْعَلِيمُ﴾

[197] al-Ḥurr al-ʿĀmilī, Shaykh Muḥammad, *Wasāʾil al-Shīʿah*, Vol. 5, p. 204.

[198] Ibid., p. 247.

*﴾idh qālati mra'atu 'imrāna rabbi innī nadhartu laka mā fī baṭnī muḥarraran fa-taqabbal minnī innaka anta s-samī'u l-'alīmᵘ﴿*

*﴾When the wife of 'Imrān said, 'My Lord, I dedicate to You in consecration what is in my belly. Accept it from me; indeed You are the Hearing, the Knowing'﴿*[199]

And God's ﷻ reward to her was for her request to be granted, and for her Progeny to be blessed through her daughter Maryam ﷺ, and her grandson 'Īsā ﷺ in return for this blessed intention. And so what prevents this blessing from including everybody who has asked God ﷻ truthfully to give them the fortune of serving in one of His sanctuaries?

God ﷻ has prevented His servants from degrading themselves, even praising the poor person who conceals their poverty to the extent that the uninformed think they are actually rich. And so if a needy servant is in need somewhere to go, they should look no further than the mosque, for it is the house of God ﷻ, and those most deserving of His aid are those dedicated to jamā'ah prayer. And that is what happened in the time of the Holy Prophet ﷺ, where the beggar went to the mosque, and was bequeathed the ring of Amīr al-Mu'minīn ﷺ who was in his rukū', triggering the revelation of a Holy Verse that will be forever recited and remembered.

---

[199] Sūrat Āl 'Imrān, Verse 35.

# The Inner Etiquettes of Jamāʿah Prayer

One of the values of jamāʿah prayer is the respect for mosques, for jamāʿah is normally performed in the mosque, and God ﷻ likes to see His house full and lively. For this reason, if the legislative ruler notices a neglect in Ḥajj one year, for example, due to a shortage of pilgrims, he sends someone to lead the prayer in al-Masjid al-Ḥarām so that it does not become vacant of worshippers. Furthermore, God ﷻ rewards the worshippers in jamāʿah based on the prayer of the best of them, contrary to the jamāʿah leader, who should take into consideration the prayer of the weakest of them. For God ﷻ showers everybody standing before Him with His mercy and generosity on the scale of the closest of their prayers to acceptance.

Faithful servants must be honest when judging themselves. And so they should not allow anybody to lead their prayer unless they have made certain that the person is righteous and dutiful. In fact, if they allow somebody to lead the prayer while there is somebody more knowledgeable between them, they are included in the Holy Prophet ﷺ's threat:

> Whoever leads a group in prayer and in them there is someone more learned than him, their affair does not cease to be towards abasement to the Day of Resurrection.[200] Therefore, all material qualifications

---

200 Ṣadūq, Shaykh Muḥammad b. ʿAlī, *Man Lā Yaḥḍuruh al-Faqīh*, Vol. 1, p. 378.

> are dropped when it comes to the leader of jamāʿah. And that applies to those praying behind the leader too, as it is mustaḥabb for the first row to be comprised of honorable servants, the criteria of which are in knowledge, righteousness, intellect, piety, and devotion.

Some of us disregard jamāʿah prayer, even when it may be beside their house or at their place of work, with the excuse that jamāʿah is mustaḥabb, or that praying alone is closer to sincerity, or that it is farther away from riyāʾ, or the obsessive doubts in the recitation or dutifulness of the leader of the prayer. In reality, the importance of jamāʿah prayer and the insistence on performing it exceed all of that and are more worthy of care than these excuses. Witness to this is what Ṣāḥib al-ʿUrwah said when talking about jamāʿah prayer:

> And there is so much emphasis on its distinctions, and admonishment of those who neglect it, in the narrations, that it almost labels it as obligatory.[201]

Some of the things made favourable in jamāʿah prayer are the straightening of the rows, closing the gaps in between, and standing shoulder to shoulder, all of which are a display of unity from the faithful society, shown by the perfection of the rows and the lack of class disparity.

---

[201] al-Yazdī, Sayyid Muḥammad Kāẓim, *al-ʿUrwat al-Wuthqā*, Vol. 3, p. 111.

Indeed, the sight of the many shoulders together is a poignant scene of camaraderie and solidarity.

Islām wishes for us to encourage children to attend the mosque and pray jamāʿah there, to accustom them to the atmosphere of group worship, for that is what ensures their faithfulness when they grow older. What bears witness to this is the scholars' verdict of allowing a child to pray in jamāʿah if he is mumayyiz (aware of the difference between right and wrong), in addition to the verdict verifying children's worship if performed correctly, just like adults'.

Being far from centres of knowledge weakens faith and prevents the acquisition of religious education, while living in remote areas inhibits the servant's ascension in both theoretical and practical senses. It is mentioned as among the conditions of the leader of jamāʿah that he should not be Aʿrābī, meaning a desert-dweller. And from this context comes the prohibition of what is known as Taʿarrub baʿd al-Hijrah, which is travelling to places where the believer cannot guarantee the security of his faith.

One of the major factors in societal growth, across all its dimensions, is the intermingling of ideologies, the sharing of cultures, and the blending of emotions. And this is achieved only through the societal gatherings mandated by Islām, such as group worship, including Ḥajj, jamāʿah prayer, Friday prayers, and ʿĪd prayers. For a long time, believers have shown kindness in these environments. At the same time, the lost have been guided, the needy have been supplied, and so many other blessings have been bestowed that are not accomplished through solitary worship.

Those lacking the trait of ʿAdālah must work very hard to attain that attribute, to access its benefits, such as: the ability to lead prayer with his family and children at home, or the ability to lead a group of believers in prayer if needed, so they do not need to pray alone, all in addition to the many privileges he will attain on the Day of Judgement, for it is narrated that the Holy Prophet ﷺ said:

> God—the Honourable, the Exalted—will put His Shade over seven people on the day in which there is no shade except for His Shade: just leaders; young people who have grown up in the worship of the Honourable the Exalted God; men whose heart is with the mosque, when they leave it until they return to it...[202]

It is advised that those tasked with leading the prayer not take notice of those praying behind him, as doing so may give him a sense of arrogance and self-importance due to their number. This may cause his prayer to vary in sincerity depending on the number of worshippers behind him, and he may take extra steps to show his devoutness, or prefer one mosque over another for a material reason. He may deem the gathering of people behind him for prayer a qualification in his favour for some worldly nobility. He

[202] al-Ḥurr al-ʿĀmilī, Shaykh Muḥammad, *Wasāʾil al-Shīʿah*, Vol. 5, p. 199.

may even take the jamāʿah prayer itself as a profession to rest his conscience, considering it a big favour to religion. In reality, there is no difference between him and the worshippers behind him in terms of the actual upholding of prayer.

The leader of jamāʿah combines two different merits, one of them being his ʿAdālah outside the prayer, and the other being that he is at the forefront of the group of believers in prayer, therefore having a right upon them, which is what Imām Zayn al-ʿĀbidīn ﷺ said in his *Risālat al-Ḥuqūq* (Treatise of Rights). And it is from here that we see certain rulings regarding the leader of prayer that highlight his position and necessitate respect. These include: not standing ahead of him, not advancing in prayer before him, listening attentively to his recitation, and not making his voice audible, even partially.

The preacher during Friday prayers must use this sacred opportunity to raise awareness of issues that concern the entire society, while reminding them of the importance of piety and counselling them on personal matters. It is in this context that this divine gathering protects the nation from the dangers of infidels and hypocrites. What is interesting is that it is mustaḥabb for the worshipper to recite Sūrat al-Jumuʿah out loud in the first rakʿah of Ẓuhr prayer on Friday, a Sūrah which contains mention for the people who most hate the Muslims, being the Jews, and Sūrat al-Munāfiqūn in the second rakʿah, mentioning the kind who are a danger to society too, for they are the ones who diverted the nation after the passing of the Holy Prophet ﷺ. Imām ʿAlī ar-Riḍā ﵇ has pointed out these specific guidelines for the Friday preacher, as narrated:

> And inform them about what would improve their religious and worldly affairs, and inform them about the various issues and the conditions which might lead to their benefit or loss.[203]

The very specific parameters for selecting and ranking leaders of prayer when there are several of them to lead a group of worshippers truly highlight the practicality of Islām when it comes to evaluating those who associate themselves with it, for there is no differentiation between one servant and the other except through what brings distinction in reality, not superficially. The narrations have specified that the first qualification to select a leader of jamāʿah from among several equal candidates is their enjoyment of the Noble Qur'ān, then their striving for the sake of God ﷻ through migration, then their age, then their application of the traditions of Ahl al-Bayt ﵈, then their knowledge of religion.

The condition of continuity and arrangement is required in all parts of prayer, in addition to the visual organisation along the lines of jamāʿah. It is mustaḥabb to have all rows equal and straight, to close the gaps between them, to line up shoulder to shoulder, and to keep the rows close

---

203 Ṣadūq, Shaykh Muḥammad b. ʿAlī, *ʿUyūn Akhbār al-Riḍā* ﵇, Vol. 2, p. 111.

together. If Islām emphasises the importance of orderliness, even visually, in the rows of jamā'ah prayer, how about its emphasis on organisation in all other aspects of life?! An example of this is when facing the enemy, when God ﷻ says,

﴿ٱلَّذِينَ يُقَـٰتِلُونَ فِي سَبِيلِهِۦ صَفًّا كَأَنَّهُم بُنْيَـٰنٌ مَّرْصُوصٌ﴾

*﴾lladhīna yuqātilūna fī sabīlihī ṣaffan ka-'annahum bunyānun marṣūṣ^un^﴿*

*﴾those who fight in His way in ranks, as if they were a compact structure﴿*[204]

Islām is the religion of camaraderie and compassion, and one of the blessings of the legislation of jamā'ah prayer is the strengthening of this brotherhood in faith, which does not accord with someone leading the prayer of people who dislike him. This can happen when somebody unworthy is in control of a house of God ﷻ, placing at the forefront of people somebody unqualified for that position. Narrations shame this form of leadership, stating that their prayers are not accepted, such as the narration from the Holy Prophet ﷺ in which he says:

---

[204] Sūrat aṣ-Ṣaff, Verse 4.

And a prayer leader of a people, praying with them while they dislike him.[205]

Despite Ahl al-Bayt 🌸's severe refusal towards the events that happened after the passing of the Holy Prophet 🌸, which is clearly observable in the Shaqshaqiyyah sermon and the Fadakiyyah sermon, they made sure at the same time to avoid splitting up the nation in its practices, even if it was divided in ideology. And this is something they practiced during their blessed lifetimes, for we have numerous narrations instructing us to treat other Muslims with respect, kindness, and friendliness, for example, by visiting their sick ones or attending their funerals. Some of these narrations speak of and encourage attending their jamāʿah prayer, such as the narration from Imām Jaʿfar aṣ-Ṣādiq 🌸 that says:

Whoever performs prayer with them in the first row, it is as if he has performed prayer with the Messenger of God.[206]

The significance of the Friday prayer has been forgotten by so many. It is sufficient in its favour that God 🌸 described it as "remembrance of God" when commanding us to hurry to it in Sūrat al-Jumuʿah. Regardless of the jurisprudential interpretation of that command—in terms of whether it is

---

[205] Ṣadūq, Shaykh Muḥammad b. ʿAlī, *Man Lā Yaḥḍuruh al-Faqīh*, Vol. 1, p. 59.

[206] Kulaynī, Shaykh Muḥammad b. Yaʿqūb, *al-Kāfī*, Vol. 3, p. 380.

wājib or otherwise—one of the merits of this prayer is that it combines accomplishing the personal aspect of the servant's relationship with God ﷻ through the prayer itself, and accomplishing the societal aspect through the Friday sermon in which the preacher discusses the issues of the Muslims and believers.

# Glossary

The following words were mentioned throughout the book and are defined here to encourage the reader to add them to their vocabulary.

| | |
|---|---|
| Call to prayer | Adhān |
| The Hereafter | al-Ākhirah |
| The sermon preached by Fāṭimah al-Zahrā' ﷺ after the death of her father, the Prophet ﷺ, in which she mentioned her right to the land of Fadak. | al-Fadakiyyah |
| A semi-circular wall beside the Ka'bah, also known as Ḥijr Ismā'īl | al-Ḥaṭīm |
| The grave of Imām al-Ḥusayn ﷺ and its immediate surroundings | al-Ḥā'ir |
| The Sacred Mosque in Makkah, inside of which is the Ka'bah | al-Masjid al-Ḥarām |
| The 'Throne' of God | al-'Arsh |
| God is greater | Allāhu Akbar |
| The Prophet's ﷺ companions native to Madīnah | Anṣār |
| The Seven Oft-Repeated Verses, a name for Sūrat al-Fātiḥah | as-Sab' al-Mathānī |
| A stage on the Day of Judgement | aṣ-Ṣirāṭ |
| The true path | aṣ-Ṣirāṭ al-Mustaqīm |

| | |
|---|---|
| A sermon by Amīr al-Mu'minīn ﷺ found in Nahjul Balagha | ash-Shaqshaqiyyah |
| A place, after death, separating the living from the Hereafter | Barzakh |
| The rising of the souls from the grave on the Day of Judgement | Baʿth |
| In the name of God, the Most Gracious, the Most Merciful | Bi-smi llāhi r-Raḥmāni r-Raḥīm |
| The recitation of Bi-smi llāhi r-Raḥmāni r-Raḥīm | Bismillāh |
| Remembrance of God, in the context of prayer, means the recited words of each stage. | Dhikr |
| The material world | Dunyā |
| Supplication | Duʿā' |
| Islāmic jurisprudence | Fiqh |
| Ritual washing of the whole body, as prescribed by Islāmic law, is to return to a state of purity. | Ghusl |
| A narration attributed to God ﷻ, spoken to us through the Prophet ﷺ | Ḥadīth Qudsī |
| The annual pilgrimage to Makkah is mandatory once in a person's lifetime | Ḥajj |
| Praise in the context of gratitude, by saying Alḥamdulilāh | Ḥamd |

| | |
|---|---|
| A person who follows the Ḥanafī monotheistic religion (not to be confused with the Ḥanafī Sunnī school of thought) | Ḥanīf |
| Prohibited | Ḥarām |
| A night in the battle of Siffin, known for the intense fighting that occurred | Ḥarīr |
| The state a pilgrim must be in to perform Ḥajj or ʿUmrah | Iḥrām |
| The position held by the 12 Imāms ﷺ | Imāmate |
| Faith | Īmān |
| The call announcing the establishment of the prayer | Iqāmah |
| Seeking forgiveness from God | Istighfār |
| The state of an act being mustaḥabb | Istihbāb |
| Seeking the right course of action from God | Istikhārah |
| The recitation of Aʿūdhu biLlāhi min ash-Shayṭān ir-Rajīm | Istiʿādhah |
| Congregational prayer | Jamāʿah |
| State of impurity caused by sexual acts | Janābah |
| Struggle in the way of God is used in both the spiritual and physical contexts. | Jihād |
| The wājib pause in the kneeling position after the second sujūd | Jilsat al-Istirāḥah |
| The state of spiritual perfection | Kamāl |

| | |
|---|---|
| A completion of the entire Qur'ān in a single time | Khatmah |
| An Islāmic tax paid on certain things, equal to one-fifth of their value | Khums |
| The exact way the letters are pronounced | Makhārij al-Ḥurūf |
| An act which is discouraged but not forbidden. | Makrūh |
| Maqām Ibrāhīm عليه السلام, located beside the Kaʿbah | Maqām |
| Mosque | Masjid |
| The Hereafter | Maʿād |
| Infallibles, in this context referring to Ahl al-Bayt عليهم السلام | Maʿṣūm |
| Rosary beads | Miṣbāḥ |
| The water spout projecting from the roof of the Kaʿbah | Mīzāb |
| An act which is allowed, neither encouraged nor discouraged | Mubāḥ |
| A whispered prayer | Munājāt |
| A duʿā' to be recited in the month of Sha'baan | Munājāt Shaʿbāniyyah |
| A recommended act, one is rewarded for their performance | Mustaḥabb |
| Plural of mustaḥabb | Mustaḥabbbaat |
| The person who recites the adhān | Mu'adhdhin |

| | |
|---|---|
| Intention is necessary before performing an act | Niyyah |
| The position held by the Prophets and Messengers ﷺ of God ﷻ | Nubuwwah |
| An act of worship performed after its set time has elapsed | Qaḍāʾ |
| A prayer shortened during travel | Qaṣr |
| The direction of the Kaʿbah | Qiblah |
| The standing position during the prayer | Qiyām |
| Another name for Ṣalāt al-Layl | Qiyām al-Layl |
| A stage in the second rakʿah of prayer involving raising hands in supplication | Qunūt |
| The intention of gaining proximity to God ﷻ through an act | Qurbah |
| A cycle of actions performed in prayer, the number of which differs depending upon the prayer | rakʿah |
| Ostentation | Riyāʾ |
| The act of bowing in prayer | Rukūʿ |
| The act of prostrating in prayer | Sajdah |
| A mustaḥabb sujūd performed in thanks to God ﷻ | Sajdat ash-Shukr |
| The greeting of peace | Salām |
| A wājib prayer performed when certain natural phenomena occur | Ṣalāt al-Āyāt |

| | |
|---|---|
| A mustaḥabb prayer of 2 rakʿahs performed when in need | Ṣalāt al-Ḥājah |
| The night prayer, a highly recommended prayer mainly consisting of Shafʿ and Witr | Ṣalāt al-Layl |
| The prayer is performed over the body of the deceased | Ṣalāt al-Mayyit |
| A prayer performed on behalf of a deceased person on the night of their burial | Ṣalāt al-Waḥshah |
| Sending peace and blessings upon the Holy Prophet ﷺ and his Household ؑ | Ṣalawāt |
| A two rakʿah prayer performed as part of Ṣalāt al-Layl | Shafʿ |
| To bear witness to a certain fact | Shahādah |
| Polytheism | Shirk |
| A piece of wood from a certain tree, used to brush the teeth | Siwāk |

| | |
|---|---|
| The act of prostration | Sujūd |
| The act of prostration upon forgetting something in prayer | Sujūd as-Sahw |
| A mustaḥabb sujūd performed in thanks to God ﷻ | Sujūd ash-Shukr |
| The act of prostration upon reciting certain verses in the Noble Qur'ān | Sujūd at-Tilāwah |
| A chapter in the Noble Qur'ān | Sūrah |
| The interpretation of the Noble Qur'ān | Tafsīr |
| Another name for Ṣalāt al-Layl | Tahajjud |
| The state of purity achieved by wuḍū' or Ghusl | Ṭahārah |
| Saying "Lā ilāha illā Allāh." | Tahlīl |
| Saying "Alḥamdulilāh" | Taḥmīd |
| Saying "Allāhu Akbar" | Takbīr |
| The takbīr is recited to begin the prayer | Takbīrat al-Iḥrām |
| A prayer performed when not travelling | Tamām |
| Saying "Subḥāna Llāh" | Tasbīḥ |
| What is recited at the beginning of the third and fourth rak'ah | Tasbīḥāt |
| Certain mustaḥabb dhikr performed after prayer | Tasbīḥat az-Zahrā' |
| Reciting the testimony of faith at the end of the second and last rak'ah of prayer | Tashahhud |

| | |
|---|---|
| Sending salutations at the end of the prayer | Taslīm |
| Circumambulation of the Kaʿbah | Ṭawāf |
| Beseeching God ﷻ through those with a high status with Him | Tawassul |
| Repentance to God ﷻ | Tawbah |
| Unity of God ﷻ | Tawḥīd |
| Certain acts performed directly after prayer | Taʿqīb |
| A piece of clay prostrated upon | Turbah |
| The five fundamental beliefs of Islām | Uṣūl ad-Dīn |
| Obligatory | Wājib |
| In this context, it refers to allegiance to Amīr al-Mu'minīn ؑ | Wilāyah |
| A single rakʿah performed as part of Ṣalāt al-Layl | Witr |
| Ablution performed in preparation for certain acts of worship | Wuḍū' |
| Islāmic tax paid on certain items | Zakāt |
| Visitation to a Holy place | Ziyārah |
| Justice: performing all the obligations and avoiding prohibitions | ʿAdālah |
| Divine justice | ʿAdl |

| | |
|---|---|
| World | ʿĀlam |
| Knowledgeable | ʿĀlim |
| The 10th day of Muharram | ʿĀshūrāʾ |
| Knowledge | ʿIlm |
| The sense of self-admiration upon performing a good deed | ʿUjb |
| Pilgrimage to Makkah can be undertaken at any time of the year | ʿUmrah |

www.ingramcontent.com/pod-product-compliance
Lightning Source LLC
Chambersburg PA
CBHW020231130626
46549CB00005B/1842